"One of life's axioms is: 'Whatev   you stronger.'
I apply this to missions trips. As you will see in her journal, for Chris
Pascual, meeting the needs of the disaster-plagued people of Haiti not
only made her a better doctor, it made her a better servant of Jesus as
well."

—*Dr. Woodrow Kroll*
Back to the Bible International

"Having been in Haiti only days after the earthquake and seeing firsthand
the destruction and great need, I can certainly identify with so much of
what Dr. Chris Pascual wrote about each day. She allows the reader to see
through her eyes and feel through her heart the physical and spiritual needs
of the Haitian people. The work she accomplished in that two-week period
was significant, but the work God did in her own life was immeasurable.
Only eternity will reveal the impact she made on the lives of those she
touched in Haiti."

—*Dr. Vernon Brewer*
President and CEO, World Help, Forest, Virginia

"Dr. Pascual's experiences in Haiti are very realistic and make you
feel as though you are with her. We have all witnessed on the evening
news the devastation caused by earthquakes, etc. Our hearts ache for
the moment, but we quickly forget them. Chris felt God's call to be
part of God's heart response to the people of Haiti in the aftermath
of the earthquake, and she will never forget her experiences in Haiti.
Her medical skills and compassionate heart were combined to make a
lasting impact, indeed an eternal one, on many lives. Her humor and
humility along with God's grace and glory come through her writing
skills. Her appreciation for the various members of the body of Christ,
as well as her love for the Lord, demonstrate what God can do through
a yielded vessel.

I believe reading this journal will leave a lasting impact on your life. Some
of you will complete the journal with the thought, 'I can do that—I want
to go on a short-term missions trip,' and your life will . . . never be the same
again. Reading the journal brought back many memories of what I have

seen in over fifty countries around the world these last forty-six years. It's good to be reminded, because we are quick to forget."

—*Dr. Harry E. Fletcher*
Vice President, International Ministry and Pastoral Care
Good News Jail and Prison Ministry

"Join Dr. Christine Pascual on the journey of a lifetime! I pray that you will seriously digest every word of her excellent journal and become awakened to the heartbreaking realities of her experiences. Hopefully, you will allow God to open doors of help through you to people in need."

—*Dr. Malcolm B. Stuart*
Retired, North American Mission Board, SBC

)

OUT OF MY

COMFORT

ZONE

A Journey into the
Medical Mission Field of Haiti

DR. CHRISTINE PASCUAL

CROSSBOOKS
PUBLISHING

CrossBooks™
A Division of LifeWay
1663 Liberty Drive
Bloomington, IN 47403
www.crossbooks.com
Phone: 1-866-879-0502

First published by CrossBooks 04/10/2012

ISBN: 978-1-4627-1467-4 (sc)
ISBN: 978-1-4627-1466-7 (hc)
ISBN: 978-1-4627-1465-0 (e)

Library of Congress Control Number: 2012906520

Printed in the United States of America

To Ed.
For never giving up on me.
For never giving up on us.

"He heals the brokenhearted and binds up their wounds."

—Psalm 147:3

CONTENTS

ACKNOWLEDGMENTS

Although I realize that the temptation to skim across the words of an acknowledgment can be great, let me ask you to reconsider as I briefly and genuinely thank a few of my favorite people in the world:

Thank you, Franklin Graham and Samaritan's Purse. Your vision of what it means to serve Christ shines in everything you do. You have brought that vision to life for me.

Thank you, faculty and students of the Great Commission Schools. Although you were not aware, it was *you* who inspired me to pursue this publication. Every penny earned by this book goes to you. I believe in who you are and what you are becoming. Keep Christ at your core. Allow Him to determine every move you make and stay in constant forward motion with Him. Obey Him and be awed by His blessings.

Thank you, Pastor Daren Ritchey and Grace Bible Church. The phrase "church family" does not begin to encompass who you are to me. Thanks for your constant support, encouragement, and love for me and my family. I hope that before I am finished here on earth, I can give you back a fraction of what you have given me.

Thank you, Mainline Medical Associates. You are not merely a business. You are a family, and one that I am proud to be a part of. Don't stop putting the patient first; it's what sets you apart. And Holly, you are a spectacular person and nurse. Thank you for every blessed thing you do for me and for our practice. I don't know what I would do without you.

Thank you, Mom and Dad. Your love and encouragement reaches beyond any words I can find. Dad, I know you are up there waiting for me, but I still miss you every day. Mom, you have been faithfully praying for me since before I was born and have never stopped. You personify love to everyone. Thank you for being the first person God chose to introduce me to His Son.

Thank you, Dave. You are the most remarkable big brother; everything you touch turns to gold. You have inspired me without knowing it for years. So I'm telling you now: I love you, and I think you are an amazing person.

Thank you, Rachel and David. You are God's faithful answers to the earliest prayer I can remember as a little girl. Love God, and love others. Do it purposefully and with passion. And far surpass your mom in your faith, wisdom, and obedience to Jesus. Be unstoppable for Him.

Thank you, Ed. You are my husband, eternal encourager, and best friend. You have shared in my successes and failures and prayed me through both. And you have loved me when this life thing has been just plain hard. You are 2 Corinthians 5:17 come to life, and I love you. Tag . . . you're it!

Thank you, my Lord and Savior, Jesus Christ. Your Name is strewn throughout this journal because it was You who were brought to my mind and heart as I walked among Your people. I pray that You would flow right out of these pages and into the heart of their reader. May Your will be done with these words. For You are the Great Author.

INTRODUCTION

January 12, 2010, was a day like any other for me. Although I don't recall the morning exactly, I can tell you it likely consisted of the following: I got out of bed at 6:35 a.m. after hitting my snooze at least a half dozen times, greeted my husband (a much better morning person than his wife), and then started the hot water for my shower. My sleepy daughter and son reluctantly got ready for school that morning with a great deal of encouragement and were driven there by my husband who had a 9:30 dentist appointment right down the street. I drove to work as always, spending some time talking with the Lord in the car while eating my traditional breakfast: banana, granola bar, and skim milk. I prayed for my staff and partners, my family, and my day, asking Him to once again "hold me together." My day went by quickly as I saw a full schedule of patients, and I skipped lunch so I could be on time as I started my afternoon session. Then, at 4:53 p.m., as I was likely seeing my last patient for the day, two blocks of earth 1,550 miles away suddenly slipped past one another, causing an earthquake. I felt nothing. I continued to stress about running at least thirty minutes behind schedule and worried about how I would fit homework, piano lessons, and dinner into what remained of the evening.

I wonder if you can recall that day with me. Although there have been quite a few natural disasters to keep track of recently, this is one you may remember. Turning on your evening news or looking online, you likely saw what I saw. The information given at first by the media meant little:

> *7.0 magnitude, earthquake's epicenter struck approximately fifteen miles west of the capital of Haiti, Port au Prince, and its two million inhabitants . . .*

But what did that mean? Soon the photos answered our questions all too well. It meant the unimaginable for those of us whose worst part of the day was catching a red light at an inopportune time. It meant pandemonium, terror, anguish, and eventual mass graves for those at the epicenter. These words, granted, are in our dictionaries, but few of us understand them. Even fewer have experienced just *one* to its fullest. Yet we all saw the videos and photos. My reaction was similar to yours: I looked at those images on the news, and my heart ached for the Haitian people. But what definitively gripped me was an online news article that featured photos of the children. That did something to me. You see, my eyes had seen their faces before. I had served in Haiti for a month in 1993 while in medical school. Back then, those faces were just as precious, but now when I looked, I could glance behind them in those pictures and see the rubble and dust that used to be their school. *Then* they were poor; *now* they were absolutely destitute. Something happened to me that day which could only have come from the heart of God—and He said, "Go."

So I did. I chose to serve through Samaritan's Purse (SP), a nondenominational Christian organization. SP provides international relief in the form of spiritual and physical aid to victims of war, poverty, natural disaster, and disease. As you know, there were many organizations who have helped in Haiti, but few that have had a lasting effect. Because SP incorporates the hope of Christ in everything they do, I wanted to be a part of that kind of effort; one that would offer eternal significance.

I recall sharing my initial thoughts with my husband. You must understand that I have known this man for twenty-three years now, and he never ceases to amaze me. He is my dearest friend and always brings out the best in me. I could barely imagine going on this trip without him and our two little ones. I explained what the Lord had placed on my heart and shared with him the fact that I felt torn between here and there. His answer was simply to hold me and say, "When God speaks to your heart, you have to obey Him. Chris, you *need* to go. We'll be fine." I soon completed an application to SP's medical missions branch, World Medical Missions, and waited for an answer. In the meantime, I invited a dear friend, Lisa, to join me in my adventure. Several weeks later, SP had approved us both, and I had a traveling partner. Lisa is a registered nurse with a diverse professional background, but more importantly, she has a tender heart for the Lord. She is a great storyteller, and her smile and laugh are contagious; I made a wise choice. Another precious friend is Shannon, who is the chair of our church's mission board. She arranged for extra funds to be given toward our traveling costs and supplies. She was also responsible for the most precious bon voyage gift imaginable—organizing the church to pray for us around the clock in fifteen-minute increments during our entire two week trip. What a blessing our church family was for us!

So that brings us to this book. Actually, it's not really a book at all; it's a journal. And I am not an author; I'm a doctor. And this wasn't meant for publication; it was just supposed to be a way for me to get my feelings out on paper. I must confess, the first entry was written on a paper napkin and a piece of scrap paper because I didn't bring a computer. It wasn't until the third day that I borrowed a laptop so I could send my thoughts to a few family members and friends to keep in touch a little. The email list soon grew, and I realized that many people at work, home, church, and beyond were suddenly traveling along with me. They kept me encouraged and loved me from miles away. So much for original intentions. What you are reading is simply my attempt to make sense of the tragedy we all saw on the news. It just so happens that I was sent to see it for myself, to breathe in the stenches, to look into the eyes of the hurting, and to touch the flesh of the wounded. And remember, I was just one of thousands who responded worldwide with compassion in the form of funds, service, and prayer. I just happened to write it down.

By the way, I ask you to consider as you read the words on the following pages that at the time I was writing them, I had no idea *you* would ever read them. Therefore, like it or not, you are about to read it in its raw form. Perhaps if I knew my journal would end up in your hands, I may have written it differently. I think that's why publication was the furthest thing from my mind as these words were penned. The Lord wanted me to be candid, open, and sincere. Otherwise, I probably would have somehow turned it into being all about me. Let me make this clear: *it is not.*

So as you go about your day today, I will join you in waking up a little later than we would like, wondering what we will have on our sandwich at lunch, and complaining that gas is too expensive. And as we go through our typical day, I will thank you for finding time in your busy schedule to read my "book." Whether you purchased it, were given it as a gift, or found it in a garbage heap, God has placed it in your hands. I've already prayed for you, so let's see what God will whisper to your heart as I share with you what He taught me as He led me out of my comfort zone.

FRIDAY, JUNE 18, 2010

ALTHOUGH OUR PHYSICAL journey begins today to Port au Prince, God's planning, as always, began long ago. Not only did He allow both Lisa and me like-mindedness on our desire to go, but our busy schedules, finances, and trip planning fell into place divinely. To prepare, I have been shopping for strange items: Crocs® (ew), DEET spray (what strength?), Silly Bandz® (thanks Jamie and Missy), and a personal stash of toilet paper. I have been trying to learn Creole on CD, emailing people all over the country, and praying about the unknown the best I can. And although God has certainly been moving, this week He let me catch a glimpse of His motion.

When I checked my email Sunday evening, I was made aware of new information regarding the supplies at the Samaritan's Purse facilities we will be working at in Cité Soleil and beyond. Unfortunately, donations have dwindled since the earthquake, leaving the cupboards nearly bare. On Monday morning, Lisa and I began calling local pharmacies, medical supply facilities, and doctor's offices. The end result was an overwhelmingly positive response from our community to help in our efforts. Four days, little sleep, and six suitcases later, we found ourselves at the airport, taking the generosity of our surrounding counties with us. Thousands of dollars worth of medical equipment and pharmaceuticals were donated, along with heartfelt wishes of goodwill. Now, I don't know much, but I know that God could have dropped those supplies from the sky, distributing them to whomever He pleased. But He didn't. And He doesn't. He often chooses to use us, His prized creation, to do His work. And that brings us to . . . today.

We are in Miami tonight for a twelve-hour layover. Once we were on our first flight, it became apparent that we would not make our second due to a delay. After waiting in the customer service line for an hour, we were informed that we needed to run as fast as humanly possible to another gate. As we were let on that flight, literally at the last minute, the door closed behind us. We eventually made it to our hotel (with the comfiest beds in the world!) and now, it's time for sleep. Ed surprised me by making an MP3 file with a recording for each night. What a sweetie. Goodnight for now. I'm going to have dreams about where our luggage may end up.

P.S. We were not charged *any* extra for our six checked bags or for exceeding the fifty-pound weight limit for five of them. Thanks, Lord!

SATURDAY, JUNE 19, 2010

AND HERE WE are in Haiti: the poorest country in the western hemisphere, plagued by an historically corrupt government, unrelenting disease, the worst sanitation possible—and now, the victim of an earthquake. *An earthquake?!* I could barely imagine what I would see and experience on arrival. I am still unsure whether I can wrap my heart and mind around it. This morning, I woke up in a very cushy bed. Tonight I will sleep on a cot under a mosquito net in a room with a dozen other women, sweating in temperatures over ninety degrees. And the earthquake was what God used to spark my desire to do so. *An earthquake?!*

I sat beside a nurse from Florida on the plane this morning who is volunteering as part of a humanitarian medical group. All she was told was that she will be in Haiti for one week—no details on location, teams, or accommodations. At the airport, we overheard the project leader tell her group that they (about twenty-five in all) would be transported directly to a hospital. We heard him say, "Yes, you heard me correctly. The hospital is full to capacity, and there is *no* staff." Where does this happen? Where there is poverty. Where there is corruption. Where the strong oppress the weak. And where earthquakes shatter already broken lives.

As our plane began to descend, we were able to see land. Typically, this is the time when passengers begin waking up, chattering, gathering their belongings, etc. Yet this time, you could have heard a pin drop. We were all mesmerized by the sights, even from so far away. Forests were stripped of their trees, piles of rubble blurred the borders of what appeared to be streets and communities, and makeshift tents were *everywhere*. Once we had landed and were waiting on the tarmac to deboard, a Haitian woman began to quietly sing a song in Creole. It was beautiful but haunting. And then she began to pray. She prayed to the One who can give hope and healing in the midst of disaster.

When we arrived at the airport, our luggage, alas, did not arrive with us. We took our carry-ons and met up with our Samaritan's Purse (SP) team. They assured us that our luggage would eventually make it. Who cares about our luggage? We want those meds and supplies! Yet I must believe that the same One who orchestrated the collection of that precious cargo will deliver it. And so, we will wait.

When we arrived at the compound, we met Kim (our interim medical coordinator) and got the tour of this oasis of God's provision. It is a sixty-six-acre facility that is home to SP's missionaries to Haiti, as well as their long-term (three to twelve months) and short-term staff (that's us). Kim and her husband will be here for one year. Their "house" is a twelve by twelve foot, wooden box with a tin roof and plastic sheets for walls. Kim is sweet, smart, and fully committed to the cause of Christ. Her husband Preston is a pilot—quick-witted and eager to serve as well. There are also many other volunteers here with various ministries, including debris removal, food and water distribution, shelter construction, and administration. I'm told that our medical director, Dr. Kara, will arrive back here about halfway through our stay. This week, there are eight on our team. I've met five so far.

One of our crew is Dr. Trey. He is a retired OB/GYN physician from Baton Rouge. He is a happy-go-lucky sort who needed to retire due to osteoarthritis. His hands have nodes all through them, and he has had both hips replaced, but he hasn't stopped. In fact, he was just here in May! He described his experiences in the Cité Soleil clinic and has begun to prepare us for security concerns. He said there have been kidnappings, riots, and many more vehicle accidents since the earthquake, especially in the city. Samaritan's Purse has been working on establishing a mobile clinic. I'm told that Lisa and I will be on that team. We start Monday. The four nurses are sweet and enthusiastic. They come from Florida and North Carolina and are also eager to help.

But work for me began today. After Lisa and I had unpacked, Kim came to find me with those words I have heard countless times: "I wonder if you could take a look at something." A few hours later, I had diagnosed and treated a construction worker from another site. (Honey, you would have been so proud. I had the patient on the cell phone and a picture of his knee on the computer screen in front of me. I was so high-tech!) I gave the order to fly injectable antibiotics to the site (thanks to Preston), then was off to continue my orientation.

Soon there was a worker with a sinus infection who needed to be evaluated, and later I found myself injecting rabies immunoglobulin into the finger of a patient who had been bitten by a dog the night before. It was a busy day and a productive one. Rachel's dance recital was tonight, many miles away. I close my eyes and know exactly how she looked. But I still missed it.

By the way, if I may back up a minute . . . When we were sitting at our gate this morning at the airport, I couldn't help but notice a large church group who would be joining us on the flight. On the backs of their shirts was the phrase: "Ak Jezi, Ayiti Va Leve." (I know; that's what I thought.) So as I was sitting there, I overheard a teenager in the group say, "Hey, you guys, you *have* to hear this Psalm. Listen, it's really important!"

She went on to read Psalm 121 (NIV): "I lift my eyes to the hills—where does my help come from? My help comes from the LORD, the Maker of heaven and earth. He will not let your foot slip—he who watches over you will not slumber; indeed, he who watches over Israel will neither slumber nor sleep. The LORD watches over you—the LORD is your shade at your right hand; the sun will not harm you by day, nor the moon by night. The LORD will keep you from all harm—he will watch over your life; the LORD will watch over your coming and going both now and forevermore."

After she had read those words aloud, all but one of her friends seemed less than impressed and went about their conversation, seemingly unaware that the Word of their Creator had spoken. I waited for a few moments and then approached her. Now, you need to understand, this was a church group from Palm Beach, but they were a Haitian church. All of these people lived in Florida but had a Haitian heritage. I explained to her that I could not help but overhear her reading of the Psalm. I thanked her, adding, "That's really cool." I meant it. Then I asked, "By the way, what does your shirt say?" Her answer made my heart feel as if it would burst. "With Christ, Haiti will rise," she said.

I don't know why Haiti is thought to be the armpit of our side of the planet. I don't know why suffering here seems to be magnified and endless. I don't know why God would allow an earthquake of this magnitude to affect an already impoverished country. But I do know that God will bring glory to Himself and help for His children through this disaster.

An earthquake?!
Yes, an earthquake.
And with Christ, Haiti will rise.

P.S. At dinner tonight, someone ran into the cafeteria, shouting, "Come outside—you *have* to see this!" And there was the most beautiful, enormous, full, double rainbow I have ever seen, completely covering the entire compound. I can't stand it; God's blessings abound. You are glorious, my Lord!

SUNDAY, JUNE 20, 2010

I WOKE UP today with an awful sore throat and low-grade temp. Not sure what to make of it, but I washed my mosquito net (it was really dusty!), took some Ibuprofen, and decided to grin and bear it. We were told this morning that we could not get our bags until Monday. The thought of those medicines and supplies sitting in that hot, corrupt airport made me feel even sicker. Thankfully, one of our team members pulled a few strings, and before we knew it, we were headed into the city.

How humbling it is even to drive down the road here and see the devastation of many years of wear and tear on these people. Being at the airport reminded me once more of what occurs when we lose our sense of right and wrong and our hearts turn toward survival mode. The workers at the airport are just as dishonest as their government overseers. They tried to give us the wrong bags, charged us for the free carts, and threatened to tax us on our luggage. Thankfully, when all was said and done, we lugged those ridiculously heavy, beautiful bags down the street and into our vehicle. And thankfully, we had Chao with us.

Chao was our interpreter today. He is a seventeen-year-old Haitian who works for Samaritan's Purse in the shelter ministry. He lost his mother (we didn't have the heart to ask him if it was in the earthquake) and was rejected by his father. When I asked him where he was during the earthquake, he tearfully answered, "In Port au Prince." I didn't ask any more questions. His dream is to complete high school, but he needs one hundred fifty dollars to register and twenty dollars a month thereafter. I felt sick when I thought of the things I have spent twenty dollars on without even thinking. I was a little concerned that Lisa was going to try to fit him into her suitcase, so I quickly changed the subject.

I have such respect for SP's structure as well as its vision. For example, the shelter branch where Chao works involves non-Haitian workers building walls off-site for the homes in Haitian communities. Then they hire Haitian workers to assemble the homes on-site, teaching them about the basics of construction during the process. The ministry's goal is to have 7,500 homes built; they have completed about 2,200 so far.

We traveled to the town of Cabaret to visit an SP shelter-home community. This town is in the mountain region, and the community is amazing. It is made up of 1,200 homes, thirty of which were built last Friday! Latrines are built every few rows, and each house, though modest, accommodates one family. The people there are genuinely happy and praising God for His provisions. Their children ran up and down the "streets" between homes, laughing and playing. Some families were beginning to plant gardens, level their small plots of land, and even build "porches" from anything they could find. They were so proud to show us their new homes.

On the way back, I asked Chao if the people of Haiti were bitter toward God. After all, He has allowed them to have next to nothing, and insult has been added to injury in the form of natural disaster. Chao seemed puzzled by my question. He answered, "We are not angry at God. We know God loves us." Period. God loves them, and they love Him back. No strings attached. How embarrassed I was when I needed to explain that we Americans have so much and yet often blame God for many of our "misfortunes." Been there, done that. Can anyone else relate? The people I saw today were praising their faithful God for a twelve-by-twelve-foot box with a dirt floor, tin roof, plastic walls, and a trek to the bathroom. They walk a mile for their water (which they drink as well as bathe in), eat only what they can grow, and have no underwear. And yet, they have joy. Joy that I often lack (get this) because of my circumstances. Wow. I again find myself humbled beyond belief.

And then this evening, we had chapel. Tonight we caught a glimpse of Haitian worship. I'll just say this now, Shannon: I'm not sure it would be for you. ☺ A visiting church's youth choir came to sing with us, and we had a real singin'-at-the-top-of-your-lungs-raisin'-your-hands-clappin'-like-crazy worship service. Lisa said Michael would have loved it.

The kids were precious. They were full of life, and watching them brought hope to my heart once again. We were asked by their leader to pray for them, to ask the Lord to protect them and allow them to rise above their circumstances. Between tears, I prayed, "Make them wildly effective for You, Lord." How often I have prayed the same prayer for my own little ones (thanks, Beth). These kids need that too. Wow. I think my heart needs a break tonight. Time for some sleep.

P.S. Once we brought our luggage back, we showed it to the staff, and they couldn't believe their eyes. They were stunned at the amount of supplies everyone had donated—from stickers for the kids to the coveted antibiotics and everything in between. They asked how we knew just how great their need had been, and we were able to share the series of events. "This thing was blessed from the start," I told them, and they shared in our joy. We are all saying our thank-yous tonight.

MONDAY, JUNE 21, 2010

I HAVE BEEN up for sixteen hours now, fifteen of which I have been working non-stop—with the exception of quick meals and two trips to the bathroom. Now, before you go and think I'm bragging, let me just say that I am exhausted, cranky, sticky (is there a word to describe hotter than hot?), and I stink. And yet our first day in the field on this medical mission was remarkable.

Lisa and I are on the mobile clinic team. This ministry was born only a few weeks ago here in Haiti, so as you can imagine, we are still working out quite a few kinks. It is made up of three nurses (one of whom is Haitian), a Haitian physician, and me. The clinic travels to a different part of the country each day of the week and carries absolutely everything with it. Now, before you get images in your mind of a true mobile clinic, let me just say that in reality it is composed of two trucks and a bunch of hardware-store buckets filled with medical stuff. Oh, and us—the new guys. This morning we packed up our equipment and some stale bread with peanut butter on it for lunch and traveled to a community about thirty-five minutes from the compound.

When we arrived, we were greeted by the stares of over one hundred people of various ages, all waiting for us. They had been there since very early in the morning, as the schedule is "first come, first served." Lisa took on the role of our pharmacist, and she had her hands full. Vicky was in triage and prayed with every blessed soul who came through the door. Dr. Fritz and I saw more than ninety patients.

Let me just say right now that I am *waaaaay* out of my comfort zone. My office/exam room was a ten-by-ten, cinder-block room with a dirt floor and a sheet for a door. I speak to my patients, who don't know who in the world I am or have any idea of what I am saying, except through an interpreter. And I could never, *ever* have prepared myself for not only the sheer volume of patients I saw but the extent of their maladies.

I saw countless numbers of children, all of them with some degree of malnourishment and dehydration, and many diseases that I have never seen or treated before. Almost every patient had fever, abdominal pain, and a headache. Soon I found myself making diagnoses I have only read about back in the States—elephantiasis, malaria, typhoid fever, and a tracheoesophageal fistula. It made me feel as if I had never even gone to medical school. And yet God allowed me to use the skills that He has given to me through the years to put the puzzle pieces together.

The most difficult part of the day was accepting the helplessness that I felt. I told those who were dehydrated that they needed water; they had none to drink. I told those who were malnourished to eat; they had no food. I had to tell many of them over and over that we simply did not have the medicine we needed to treat their diagnosed condition. How do you treat an illness without the treatment? As I found out today, you improvise. And you pray.

One of my patients was a twenty-four-year-old woman who was two months pregnant. She already had five children and could not feed one more. So she came to me for an abortion. She had already begun a folk remedy to start the process. She wanted me to finish the job. I declined, explaining that she could continue the medicine or stop it. It was her choice. However, I said I believed that life is a gift from God and that God can make a way to accomplish the impossible if we make choices that honor Him. I said that if she decided to continue the process on her own and regretted it later, that same God would provide forgiveness and healing. I prayed with her, and she was very open to my words. (Did you ever pray while you were praying for the right words to pray?) When we were through, I said good-bye, adding, "No matter what you choose, never forget—Jesus will always love you." She smiled and said, "I know He does."

What did I do today? I'm still not sure. I made a dent in a rock so firm it would take God Himself to break it. I guess I need to remember that it's not my job to break the rock. It's His. My job is obedience. If I focus on *my* role in all of this, I defeat the purpose. If I obsess over *my* ability (or lack thereof), *my* achievements, *my* hard work, I take the glory from the One who gives me what I need to accomplish anything. So I will depend on Him to allow me to "do" what He allows me to accomplish. And I will acknowledge that every breath I breathe is a gift from Him.

I can barely recall a time when I have been so exhausted. I need a good cry. Thank you, Lord, for a remarkable day.

TUESDAY, JUNE 22, 2010

TODAY WE TRAVELED to another community to set up our clinic. This time it was at a church. We actually set up triage in the entrance, placed the physicians' "exam rooms" in the sanctuary, and plopped the pharmacy smack-dab in the middle of the altar. I know it may sound sacrilegious to some, but I think it all made God smile. The people there were so grateful to have access to health care and medicine that even their lack of privacy (let me just say that HIPAA is nonexistent here) did not seem to bother them. The church where we set up was Balthazar's church. Who is Balthazar? I'm glad you asked.

Balthazar is a thirty-something, seven-foot Haitian man who I'm glad is on our side. He serves as our security officer and driver, and he takes his job *very* seriously. He has worked for SP only four months, but you wouldn't know it. That is because everywhere you go, *everyone* knows and loves Balthazar. This is the kind of guy who enters a room and lights it up. He is a natural leader, a gifted teacher, and has a commanding presence.

Balthazar would be the first to tell you that he is nothing special. That's what makes him so endearing. He loves the Lord and gives Him the glory for every good thing in his life. He is the worship leader at his church (his father is the pastor), and he leads the children and youth choirs. He is married, with two young children. When he drove us into town, children yelled his name and ran after our van. When we arrived and unloaded the van, everyone had a hug, smile, or wave for Balthazar. He is the kind of guy you just like to be around because he makes you feel as if you are his best friend.

I asked him about his love of music. He said his ability is a gift from God, and he is honored to use it for Him. His favorite part of music ministry is leading the youth choir. He said that he has three simple rules: (1) Be respectful of time (if they are late for practice at six a.m. on Saturday, he sends them home); (2) Be respectful of others; and (3) Obey God's Word.

Oh, is that all? He is strict, and they love him for it. When I grow up, I want to be like Balthazar.

Last night we were up late, digging through all of the meds and supplies we'd brought, packing them up, and labeling stuff. That made our work much more organized today and allowed us to give more appropriate meds, vitamins, etc., to our patients. We used a donated, battery-operated nebulizer today for the first time, and I just about cried. (Would someone please thank Jessie for me?) There were three patients who came in with significantly labored breathing, who left with clear lungs and smiles on their faces.

I saw lots of scabies today, along with the usual malaria, malnourishment, dehydration, and diarrhea. There were more pregnant women, none of whom had any prenatal care or even one vitamin to take. I prayed with them—for their health, for their unborn children, and for the other little ones they had at home. So many of these people follow their complaints with, ". . . ever since the earthquake." It's almost as if they separate life into *before* and *after* the quake, because life was hard, now it is harder. The water was dirty, but now it is often nonexistent. The food was scarce, but now there is nothing to eat. And their memories haunt them. My heart is not sure what to do with that.

Yet the hope I see in our little corner of the country still shines. We were told tonight that the medical missions group in Haiti is growing rapidly. It has become so needed and so well-received by volunteers, that they are in the process of expanding it further than they had hoped. I love it, because their mission is not just to bring doctors and nurses in to see patients. They are forming teams of people to go into villages and instruct them in hygiene, disease prevention, and proper nutrition.

As the teams are teaching them to do these things, they are digging wells so people can cook with and drink clean water, and actually wash their hands with soap. The volunteers are teaching construction methods as they provide shelter and build clean bathrooms. They are removing earthquake debris so people can farm their land. Everything they do is meant to enable the Haitian people to eventually become self-sufficient.

And along the way, they are passing on the truth of God's Word and the love of Christ—but *not* as a conditional bribe or dangling carrot. It is offered as Christ Himself offered it: as a free gift for anyone who chooses it. It is a personal decision for a personal relationship with a personal God. And take it or leave it, they are still helping. WWJD? *That's* what He would do.

And now, once again, it is time for bed. I miss home so much tonight. I know that life is continuing without me just fine, but I wish I could be in *both* places. I long for hugs and kisses from the kids, curling up with Ed and talking forever, and, well, chocolate. But I am here for a reason, and that reason goes way beyond me. I will be home soon enough, and when I am, I will soak up every moment while it looks new again, before it turns back into the ordinary right before my eyes.

P.S. We were told tonight that the water used to make the juice we have been drinking from the cafeteria was recently tested and found to be "okay." Excuse me? Define *okay*. Well, it would seem that a few weeks ago, the water was found to have fecal organisms in it, and they needed to change the filtration system. Now, you have to understand that I have been so careful about stuff like this that I am using bottled water to brush my teeth. Yet I have been chugging this juice stuff like crazy. Oh, well. What doesn't kill us makes us stronger, right? Even in the world of microorganisms. I think I need a drink. ☺

WEDNESDAY, JUNE 23, 2010

AND JUST WHEN you think it can't get any busier . . . Today we traveled to a local village that is actually SP's first shelter community. We were dropped off right in the middle of the area, where "the guys" put up two large tents for us to work under. And then "the guys" left. Along with our van. Huh? Well . . . that's okay. We still had our interpreters, and there was work to be done.

At first, the system was rather orderly. The WASH team from SP had been there the day before and had given them a talk on hygiene, infection control, etc. The locals were less than impressed and did not want to attend at first. That is, until they were told that they would be first in line when the doctors got there the next day. So forty-five patients were waiting for us with bells on, bright and early this morning

While we were seeing those patients, I heard a Haitian woman yelling out some sort of message outside the tent. I asked Seraphim (my interpreter, who is awesome!) what she was saying. "She say, 'Come! Come to see doctor! Come bring you sick family and get medicine!'" Oh. (Maybe something to consider for the office, Mitch?)

Anyway, before we knew it, we were flooded with children and adults as far as the eye could see. We just put our heads down and ran with it. And then, the wind started. Picture two large, thick canvas tents with the sides tied up halfway with rope, flapping on a mountaintop with wind blowing like crazy. There was no front or back, just a wind tunnel. Dust was everywhere, and those people just kept coming.

And then the rain started.

We had heard we were in for a storm, and thankfully it didn't rain for long, but it made the above circumstances feel like, well, mass chaos!

There were children everywhere, often running into the tent, stealing water bottles from our supply. There was no room; while I was seeing one patient, the next *two* were sitting next to him or her, listening in on our little chat. There they were, nodding, adding their two cents' worth to the *other* guy's visit!

Dr. Fritz and I saw almost one hundred patients today. Lots of kids, lots of earthquake stories, lots of malnourishment and disease. If I don't have scabies by now, it will be a miracle. One little girl came up to me while we were setting up. She couldn't have been more than eighteen months old. She looked at me with those big brown eyes, with her ratty dress, dusty, dirty body, and bumps all over her skin. And then she stretched out her arms. Now you *know* what I did. I bet you would have held her too.

Toward the end of the day, I saw a two-year-old with a large abscess on her chest and a fever of 101 degrees. It was obvious the lesion needed an incision and drainage, and when I explained that to her mother, she shook her head no. You see, she had been told by others in the community that her daughter had developed this pocket of pus near her neck because she was teething. I know she didn't believe me when I pleaded with her to let me take care of it, but she ultimately gave her consent, and we prepared.

I grabbed what we had; the only scalpel was a size I didn't realize was actually manufactured for human use. We had no Betadine®, drape, culture, or packing. All we had was this jumbo scalpel, gauze, and me. Thankfully, Lisa and Vicky assisted me, and we took care of this sweet child. If they hadn't held her so effectively, I could have easily nicked that little carotid just a half a centimeter away. I'm not being dramatic. It was unlike anything I could have ever imagined doing. I had to smile, because I felt like I was on an episode of *M*A*S*H* (minus the enclosed structure, sterile conditions, and adequate medical equipment).

When it was lunchtime, all of the staff just stood and looked at one another. The Haitian SP workers said, "Go, you take break." And then we looked at all of the eyes watching us. In those open tents. Waiting for us to see them next. We just couldn't do it. It took a while to convince our interpreters that we did not need a break; they are so protective of us and our well-being. (Hmm . . . kind of reminds me of you sweet nurses back home on side A.) But we soon found ourselves completing the day's work.

Later, as we began to drive away, we noticed the bag of peanut butter sandwiches that we had neglected to eat for lunch. We looked at them and knew that they would be thrown away as soon as we got back to the compound. And then we saw the children chasing our van on our way out. We decided to toss the bag out of the window as we exited the compound.

You guessed it. Picture thirty vultures coming across an unfortunate, small animal. They tore that bag to shreds right before our eyes and devoured those sandwiches. It was every man for himself. And it was an image of what goes on every day in the world to some degree. The little ones never had a chance. The faster, older kids had dominion and used it for all it was worth. It was the perfect picture of greed. That image will be burned in my mind for quite some time.

So now I'm checking up on my e-mails from friends and family. (Please write if you want. We share a computer, but I check every day). I talked to my kids for the first time all week, and I was so thankful. Those little voices were music to my ears.

They were quick to bring me back to the reality of their lives. David couldn't wait to tell me how he had beat the portion of Lego Star Wars® that he has been diligently working on, and Rachel told me the backstage stories of her dance recital. They are in their world, and I am in mine right now. God willing, I hope to bring just enough wisdom back home with me to know when to push the point of thankfulness and when to back off. I think that we belong somewhere between extreme depravity and spoiled brat. I'm not sure that I've found my own place in that spectrum, but I am praying that God will help me to do so.

What I *do* know is that the patients I saw today will always be poor. Sure, there may be a few who will make it out. But really, let's be honest. Most of these Haitians will be born poor and die poor—some from untreated abscesses in their little necks. Their hope is not in this life. And nor is it, truly, in ours. For even if we live comfortably, what good is it in the end without the hope of an eternity with the One who made us in the first place?

So we tell these people of the One who came for us all while we were in our depraved state of sin. We tell them that we all have this garbage in our lives and that God's solution was to wrap Himself in human flesh to save us all from ourselves. We tell them that we are thankful for their gratefulness, but that only He is the Great Physician. And as we tell them about *our* dear Jesus, we tell them that He is *theirs* too. We tell them this because it's true. If it were just a nice story, I wouldn't waste my breath, and I certainly wouldn't waste it here.

Okay, enough preaching. My team tells me it's dinnertime. I wonder what tomorrow will bring.

THURSDAY, JUNE 24, 2010

I KNEW I shouldn't have done it. I just couldn't help it. I opened my e-mail tonight to write my journal entry, and I saw all of your responses waiting for me. I literally had to catch my breath when I saw that there were messages from all of you. And then I did it. I opened them. Every blessed one. The tears poured from me as I read each word; they are as sweet to me as you can imagine. I had no idea how much I am loved. I don't want to sound trite, but *thank you* with all of my heart. I needed that.

Balthazar drove us to another church today, where we set up shop. We were up at 5:00 a.m., had devotions and breakfast, and then loaded up. Ninety-seven patients later, we packed up the clinic and headed back to home base. It was a long, hard, good day. We saw a wide variety of patients today in a broad range of ages, lots of chronic diseases (right up my primary-care alley), some sick kids, and a bunch of pregnant women. I saw a woman who was in her eighth month, and I was literally (and desperately) rifling through the OB textbook in my brain, reviewing the procedure for delivery. Thankfully, I did not require those skills today.

I did diagnose a new pregnancy, though, and when I gave her the results I hesitantly asked, "Is that good news?" (In my experience, I *never* assume.) She smiled and said, "Oui." I asked if I could pray for her and her baby, and we bowed our heads to talk a little with the Creator of that brand-new life. When we finished, I asked if she would like to take the test home with her. (I had shown her the little "+" and her eyes had shone). Tears filled her eyes, and she accepted. She thanked me profusely, adding shyly that she wanted to show it to her husband. As she left the room, I winked at her and said, "That's okay, I kept mine too." Oh, how well I remember that moment when I first knew that the God of life had blessed me with a child!

I can also vividly recall losing that same precious child. Today, I met with two other women, both pregnant, both of whom had not felt movement from their unborn children in several weeks. I looked at these dear women. Their bodies visibly showed the beautiful signs of expectant motherhood, but inside there was little chance that life remained. How well I knew what the next step would hold for them—the heartache, guilt, and questions that would remain after completing the required procedure. I would like to say that I was eloquent in my heartfelt prayers for them, but the truth is, I didn't even offer to pray. I couldn't. I simply didn't know what to say. I prescribed each of them a vitamin, instructed them to see an obstetrician, and managed to get out a "God bless you." Lord, forgive me for bailing! I can now, of course, think of a hundred profoundly spiritual things I could have said, but I didn't. But I will pray for them tonight as the images of their faces still burn in my heart.

One final pregnancy story: One of my last patients of the day was yet another pregnant woman. Great with child, she waddled into my "room"—a cement-block, dirt-floor area with an old sheet hung for scant privacy. She was sweet and quiet. It was her heartburn that had motivated her to make the long walk to the doctor that one-hundred-degree day, and my heart went out to her. (Thanks to my dearest Rachel, I can relate when it comes to heartburn!) I gave her some suggestions, wrote a prescription, and wished her well. I prayed with her, being sure to include her family in the prayer, as she has four other children.

When we were through, she slowly got up, and as she was ducking under the sheet, she looked back and said something to my interpreter. I smiled. I just knew she was thanking me. He said, "She say, 'The baby's father is dead.'" Oh. My heart sank, and I was again at a loss for words.

I know all of these things happen back at home. I know all of this pain and suffering is part of a sin-ridden world. I know there was nothing I could have done to change her situation. But it just doesn't seem fair, does it? These people live a life of poverty, disease, hunger, and all other forms of suffering. And then they have to deal with this other stuff. I'm sure it won't be the last time I ask *why* in these two weeks, but it sure is a good question.

On a lighter note, the best part of my day was lunchtime. We typically break for thirty minutes in the middle of our day, so we all crammed into the van, cranked up the AC, and ate our stale peanut butter sandwiches. But today was special. Today, Balthazar bought us all Cokes®. It might as well have been something much stronger, because we all talked so loud and laughed so hard that we had tears in our eyes. I haven't laughed like that in days.

Our interpreters are all such characters, and we probably don't help matters as we egg them on. After our week thus far, that catharsis was just what the doctor ordered.

Back at the compound, we spent a couple more hours categorizing and restocking medicines. Lisa has become quite the pharmacist and was able to give useful suggestions, as Samaritan's Pure is setting up their second mobile unit to launch next week. This relief-effort medical team has taken on a life of its own, and it is amazing to see firsthand what a bunch of like-minded Christ-followers can do when given a clear mission. It's an honor to be part of it.

So my thoughts for today go to the realization that although God allows us a variety of experiences in life for many purposes, one of the primary reasons is to love one another more fully. I guess it can take the form of empathy, prompting us to carry another's emotional burden, perform an act of service, or help in any way we can. I mean, why did you e-mail me back? Because you had a time in your life when you felt lonely and far from home too.

As I think about my day in that context, I look at the fact that there have been two doctors in our clinic all week. God sends the patients He wants me to see my way, and the others go to Dr. Fritz. He can do that. He is God. And I think that one of His decision-making processes has to include the lessons He has burned into our hearts through the years of trial and error in our lives. So, it would stand to reason that the Lord calls us to do certain things and go to certain places so we can broaden our experiences and therefore help more people. Maybe that's too simple, but that's what I got from today. And maybe, just maybe, this whole helping-other-people thing has an even grander purpose. Because when we learn to love others more, we learn to love our Creator more. Maybe that's one way that He helps us to fulfill His greatest commandment. As I pore over the pages of my Bible, that's what the Lord brings to my heart. Just a thought.

P.S. Okay, thanks to the photos Lisa posted online, many of you have met our new friend, the tarantula. The construction guys found it only feet from our room. For those of you who don't know, I am deathly afraid of spiders. You know how there are certain things that when you see them on TV or flip to a picture of them, they make you want to crawl out of your skin? Yeah, well, for me, it's spiders. And for the record, Lisa was shaking and the staff was laughing at her as she took that picture. I, of course, was bravely huddled behind her. What a team we are! One of the construction crew guys told us that last week they filled a bucket with sixty of those things. I'm going to sleep *great* tonight. I think I'll go take an Ambien®.

P.P.S. I started myself on an antibiotic and am feeling much better! (Thanks for asking, Crystal. It really pays to have a stage mom. ☺)

FRIDAY, JUNE 25, 2010

THERE HAVE BEEN moments this week when I can close my eyes and be home in an instant. I immediately find myself surrounded by the sights and sounds of those people and things that I love. Today, however, I am finding it difficult to go there. Today, you all seem so very far away. I think I am officially immersed.

We visited two orphanages today. The first was in a village where we ended up seeing many people from the town in addition to the orphans who were ill. We began triage at 8:00 a.m. In the blink of an eye, it was noon, and we had seen eighty patients! Many of them were large families, and my head was spinning as I treated groups of four and five people at once under a hot plastic tent at 108 degrees. Again, the destitute condition of these people just slapped me in my rich American face.

The children often looked at us with blank stares. They were dirty and halfway naked, and many were covered with deep, infected sores from scabies. For some reason, this community seemed more desperate than the others we had seen. They pushed their way through triage, crowded around Lisa in the pharmacy, and had multiple complaints for me. Whereas the children we had seen elsewhere had often been full of life, mischievous, and affectionate, these little ones . . . well, they just seemed empty.

I saw a lot of malaria today. The kids and adults were among the sickest we have seen. Some of their fevers were so high, I could feel their skin radiate before I laid my hands on them. My office was the tent I mentioned, which had a large pile of what appeared to be garbage along one side. Upon further inspection, I discovered it was actually layers of medical supplies, clothing, and pharmaceuticals, haphazardly tossed in that space. I saw everything from Sponge Bob® pajamas to colostomy bags. I couldn't help wondering if anything would change if we returned years from now.

I mention all of this because a recurring theme we see here is that much of the country is in chaos. That, of course, extends to cities, villages, and homes. Garbage piles are everywhere, filthy markets litter the streets, traffic is a no-rules playground, and most people are unsure of their age because they do not know their birth date. So my "office" today was just an unfortunate extension of that chaos. The thing that bothers *me* is that it doesn't bother *them*. Oh, I admit it; I am Type A (as most of you know). However, consider that the God we read about in Scripture is a God of order. He has created us to maintain a certain degree of order while being flexible and creative. I saw none of this in that scene this morning.

Nonetheless, because He is God (and I certainly am not), He allowed His plan to proceed today. He allowed us to share His love, to pray with the brokenhearted, to treat their illnesses, and in some cases, to lift their spirits. As always, He is able to bring beauty from those ashes. That brings me to this afternoon . . .

Samaritan's Purse got a call last week from the director of an orphanage down the street from our compound. After further investigation, the site was approved and cleared for a medical visit. Today our team served there for the first time. We traveled a few back roads. (God bless Balthazar. How *does* that man maneuver the van around those streets?) Goats, dogs, and children were everywhere. Whereas we used to snap multiple photos as we witnessed such sights, now we watch them go by as commonplace occurrences: Oh, yeah, there's a woman taking a bath in the river . . . Yup, there are two boys having a peeing contest on the side of the road . . . There's a guy with two stalks of bananas on his head.

Anyway, when we got to the orphanage, the village children began their familiar chant of "Blan, Blan, Blan!" ("white"). The gate closed behind us, and we found ourselves in . . .

. . . a haven.

This small orphanage was started by a Haitian professor with a big heart for kids and a bigger heart for Christ. He is responsible for fifteen children who range in age from five to thirteen years old. They were all clean, well-behaved, and awfully excited to see us. What they didn't know was that we couldn't wait to see them either.

After the morning we'd had, these children were a breath of fresh air to me. There they were, all waiting patiently in a row, each holding a registration paper. They giggled quietly and pointed at us as we unloaded our van.

And then we got out the Silly Bandz®. You would have thought it was Christmas. They looked at them with wonder, compared shapes with each other, and gave us all hugs. After we gave them out, I saw another little boy to whom I offered a band. He did not accept. I was taken aback until he reached out his arm. He revealed that his wrist already had a band on it. He was so honest in showing me that he had already received the gift, that I just had to give him another. He smiled as he said, "*Mèsi*."

Later, I took my own tour of the humble facility and gained further insight to the boy's honesty. Now, you might argue that this was just a good kid. Maybe before his parents died, they had taught him right from wrong. Or maybe he was afraid he would get in trouble if he lied. I would say that the truth lies in what I saw in those primitive rooms. There were signs of Christ *everywhere*—from the Sunday School books in the classroom, to the mural made up of all of their little handprints in a large cross shape, to the Bible verses posted on the cinder-block wall. I believe he chose to do what is right because he has learned that it is what Christ would have done. I guess you'd have to ask him, but that kid didn't hesitate. And I think he made Jesus smile.

On the way home, I read the profiles of each of these precious souls. The words still haunt me: ". . . abandoned by her mother . . . found on the streets without care . . . parents died in the earthquake . . . forced into slave labor . . . aunt could no longer feed him . . ." Tears welled in my eyes, just as they are in many of yours.

These are real kids. I held them today. I listened to their hearts, touched their little school desks, and returned their genuine smiles. And then, praise God, I read more of their stories: ". . . chose Christ as his Savior . . . wants to be a seamstress when she grows up . . . the boys welcomed him in as a brother . . . she tells the other girls about Jesus . . . he wants to become a pastor . . ." They are safe, they are loved, they have a home, and they have an opportunity to fulfill their dreams.

And they have guidance from the One they call Lord. Make no mistake, their faith is genuine. They are the real deal. Oh, if my faith and walk could be so pure! I'm not saying that these little ones are perfect. I'm saying that they have simple faith and hope in a God who loves them. I'm saying that although they are just learning how to read, they are working their way through the same Bible verses that I read. They will no doubt be taught to cling to the Author of that Book as they go through this arduous life they have each been given. And despite the fact that our lives are worlds apart, their God is my God—and I need to cling just as tightly to Him as I walk my road.

P.S. Something wonderful happened today. It is one of the most beautiful things I have ever witnessed. Last week, the medical team that was here before us had noticed a little boy who would stand at our gate every morning. He was clothed only with a dirty T-shirt—nothing from the waist down. They befriended him and found out that he had been forced into slave labor. The only thing he knew about himself was his name. His mother had included it on the box she had left him in after he was born: Yo jwenn ("they find"). He broke that team's heart, and they asked SP if there wasn't *something* that could be done for him.

We were told at devotions this morning that, after further investigation, our guards were planning to take him from his owners and rescue him. We prayed like crazy and then left for our day. When we returned, we found out that he had been successfully rescued and given a bath, medicine, and a new set of clothing. Plans are in motion for a meeting with the judge tomorrow to attempt custody of Yo jwenn. If the judge rules in favor of SP, they will hand him over to a trusted orphanage that will ensure his complete education and welfare.

I was a mess when I heard the story. And then I met Yo jwenn. He is the sweetest thing you ever did see. He was welcomed into our compound with the full love of Christ, and although you might think he would have been overwhelmed, he soaked it in like a dry sponge. He snuggled up when we hugged him, smiled from ear to ear when we took his picture, and ate two platefuls of dinner and drank three glasses of Gatorade® and a Sprite®. I know because I cut up his meat and fed it to him. He was like a baby bird with his mama. He devoured that food! It was the perfect picture of how Christ rescued me from my own desperate state. Oh, who would I be without Him?

Lisa just came in and said that she saw him with Rick, the staff member in charge of his rescue. Rick was to leave Haiti today but delayed his flight home to take care of Reginald. Oh, did I mention? Rick changed the boy's name to Reginald. No longer will he carry the stigma of being left. He has been found. But instead of "they" finding him, God's people found him. We cried out to Him on behalf of one of the least of these, and He said yes. I know there are thousands of Reginalds in Haiti. But tonight, one of them sleeps safely at our home base in a fresh set of pj's, under a mosquito net, and with a full belly. *Thank you, God, for saving Reginald. Thank you, God, for saving me.*

SATURDAY, JUNE 26, 2010

IT IS 4:00 p.m. yet it is still a sweltering 101 degrees. And although the sun is shining bright, it was a dark day for me.

I don't want to be pessimistic, but things just got to me today. We headed out to a large orphanage this morning that was on the other side of Port au Prince. This meant that we needed to drive through Cité Soleil. We had only seen the outskirts of the city on the day we arrived. I knew that things would look worse today compared to my last visit here. But that was 17 years ago. That was before the earthquake.

As we drove from our small oasis in the mountains, the sights gradually became more grotesque and destitute with each mile we traveled. Soon we were in the thick of the city. It was then that I remembered. (Jake, I know you remember too). I remembered the degree of filth. I remembered the heaps of garbage everywhere. I remembered the water mixed with sewage running down the middle of the street with children wading in it, people bathing in it, and dogs eating out of it. The only thing that kept me from losing it was that I was snapping photos, attempting to capture those images as best I could. Two hours later, we arrived at the orphanage and began to unpack.

We were told that we would see about thirty-five children today and would not need much in the form of medicines. These would be well-child checkups—a refreshing change from the pathology we have seen up to this point. We entered the gate to find 102 unruly children who seemed to be as surprised about our presence as we were with their numbers. None of them had registration papers, and there were no adults with them who spoke English. We had only brought two interpreters with us, yet we had three doctors and three nurses. It was a zoo. I spoke more Creole today than I have in my life, and I missed Seraphim desperately!

31

Eventually we were able to access one of the helpers from the orphanage who spoke enough English to get by, and we got started. We had only a handful of "well" children among those we treated. These kids were not well-cared-for like those we had seen yesterday. The difference was like night and day. I don't know what their spiritual food may have been, but there was no clear sign of the Lord's presence in that place. These kids were not only poor, they were poor in spirit.

The last straw was when we passed out the Silly Bandz®. You guessed it—we got mobbed. It wasn't pretty. The older kids pushed the little ones so they could be first. Many would come back to us, hiding the bands they had already received, leaving others with nothing. The principal of the orphanage showed up toward the end of our visit. I found it particularly interesting that he failed to pitch in and help interpret. In fact, as he stood back and watched these kids cave in to their greed, he did nothing.

We packed up as soon as we could. We were hungry, thirsty, tired, and discouraged. And then we headed back through the city.

This time I was too tired to take any pictures, so I had more time to just "sight-see." I began to feel physically ill as I watched those sights go by: people bathing out of a small stream of water in the middle of the street, extraordinary amounts of debris from toppled buildings, thick mounds of garbage right next to food stands. I would love to tell you that I closed my eyes and cried out to God in intercessory prayer for them. But I didn't. I just plain lost it.

Lisa caught me in the middle of my silent tears. They just kept streaming down my face. I did my best to explain my behavior. "It's not fair," I managed to squeak out. But in my heart, I was screaming, *It's not fair!* It's not fair that they were born here! It's not fair that they have to live here! It's not fair that they have nothing that is pretty, nothing that is clean, nothing that safely belongs to them!

And here I am, telling dehydrated patients that they need to drink more water: *from the filthy liquid I saw today?* I am telling them to eat more meat for protein and fruits and vegetables for vitamins: *from the rotting, foul-smelling, roadside selection I saw today?* Wash your hands? They have no hope for sanitation in that city under those conditions, and rampant spread of disease is the natural result. And don't get me started on the number of homeless, abandoned children we saw strewn across those miles. It was beyond heartbreaking. There are just no words for what we saw today.

Now, aren't you glad you are reading my journal? What do we do with this? Because whether we see this stuff in person or not, it is still there. *It is real.* From the streets of Bangladesh to the slave markets of the Sudan lie the unsightly circumstances we would all rather forget at times. Haiti is no different, but my heart, of course, is here. Guess what. We are not *supposed* to think it's fair, because it's not. As Mom always said, life isn't fair. Jesus implied it too when He reminded us that the poor would be with us always. At first glance at those Scriptures, I kind of feel like saying, "Yeah, thanks a lot for the reminder, Lord!"

But then I pause and say, "Yes. Thanks for the reminder." Because from the realization of that truth comes a host of emotions and subsequent actions that He wants to stir up in us. It brings forth compassion that, by definition, drives us to help. It makes us desperately thankful for what we have, no matter what our circumstances. It compels us to think of others and get our minds off of ourselves. I don't know about you, but I need a heavy dose of that at times. I am crying again. I just can't shake those images. And do you know what? I hope I never do.

P.S. Reginald's custody was officially turned over to Rick by the judge today. It cost him two hundred dollars to literally buy that little one. The woman who was using him to work was at the hearing. She took her money and never turned back. Before she left, an SP worker asked her, "Aren't you going to miss him?" She abruptly said, "No." And that was that.

Tonight, he will sleep safe and sound in an orphanage down the road from us. Rick decided to make his middle name Moses, for obvious reasons (I think it's "Moyiz" in Creole), and Reginald now has Rick's last name. After Rick discussed it with his wife, who is back in the states, they decided to begin the process for adoption, which will likely take about six months.

Meanwhile, he will be well-fed, well-schooled, and given a firm foundation of the teachings of Christ as he is shown His love. Actually, in these last twenty-four hours, he has been given quite a dose of that. When I saw him this morning, his eyes lit up (he probably thought, "Look! The meat lady!"), and he gave me a huge hug. Little did I know that it would be the highlight of my day. Thank you, Lord, for Reginald and for the lessons you are teaching me through him.

A Firsthand View of the Post-Earthquake Devastation in the Port au Prince Area (Images 1-6)

Our oasis in the mountains: a side view of the Samaritan's Purse compound

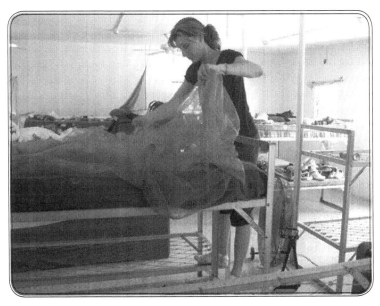

"This morning, I woke up in a very cushy bed. Tonight I will sleep on a cot under a mosquito net in a room with a dozen other women, sweating in temperatures over ninety degrees." Here I am trying to figure out my mosquito net.

"The people I saw today were praising their faithful God for a 12' x 12' box with a dirt floor, tin roof, plastic walls . . . I again find myself humbled beyond belief."

"Their children ran up and down the 'streets' between homes, laughing and playing . . ." Vicky and friends at SP's Cabaret shelter community.

"Some families were beginning to plant gardens, level their small plots of land, and even build 'porches' from anything they could find. They were so proud to show us their new homes."

"I love the fact that our team does not harp on the titles of 'doctor' or 'nurse' . . . each of us has been seen helping in the pharmacy, stocking empty shelves, and taking out the garbage. No one is 'better' than anyone else."

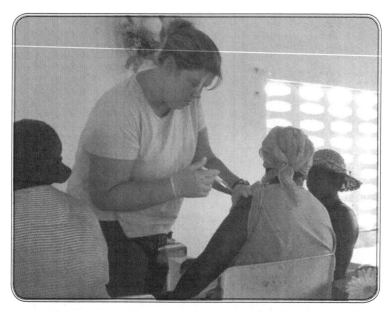

Lisa administering an injection in the first week of our mobile clinic. Due to the lack of privacy, this shot was given in the arm. (Ouch!) In the States, it would have been given in the . . . well, I think you can guess!

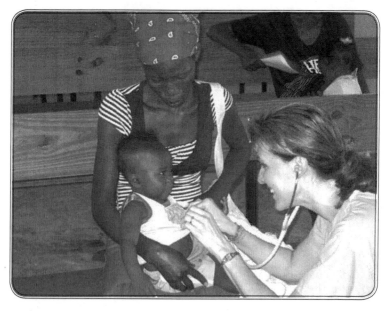

I'm not sure who made whom smile first, but it was a delight to care for these little ones!

Praying (with Seraphim's help) for this woman who came in with an asthma attack. Thanks to a donated, battery-operated nebulizer (Jessie, you're a gem), in minutes her breathing was no longer labored, and she walked home with a smile.

"We actually set up triage in the entrance, placed the physicians' 'exam rooms' in the sanctuary, and plopped the pharmacy smack-dab in the middle of the altar . . . I think it all made God smile."

"When I grow up, I want to be like Balthazar."

"How humbling it is even to drive down the road here and see the devastation these many years of wear and tear have had on these people."

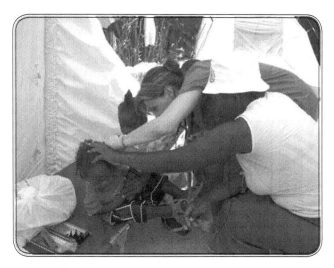

My mother told me that I put my pediatrician through
similar rigors when I was a young patient. It took great
effort from us all to get a peek in this little guy's ear.

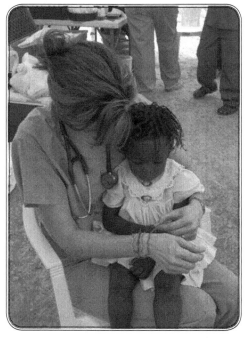

"She looked at me with those big brown eyes, with her ratty dress, dusty, dirty
body, and bumps all over her skin. And then she stretched out her arms. Now
you *know* what I did. I bet you would have held her too."

"Thankfully, Lisa and Vicky assisted me, and we took care of this sweet child. If they hadn't held her so effectively, I could have easily nicked that little carotid just a half a centimeter away."

"Most . . . will be born poor and die poor—some from untreated abscesses in their little necks. Their hope is not in this life. And nor is it, truly, in ours."

"I saw countless numbers of children, all of them with some degree of malnourishment and dehydration, and many diseases that I have never seen or treated before."

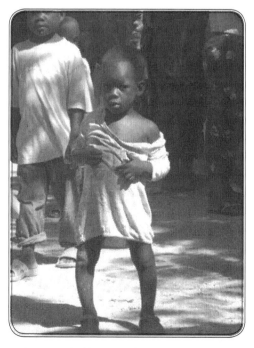

"They were dirty and halfway naked, and many were covered with deep, infected sores from scabies . . . Some of their fevers were so high, I could feel their skin radiate before I laid my hands on them."

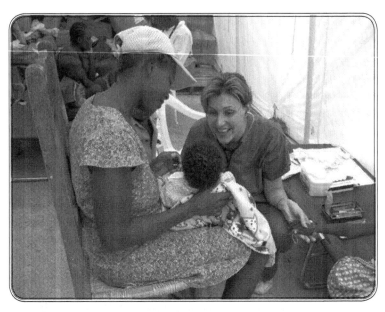

This little boy reminded me of my son back home. I love how his sister (sitting to his right) didn't want me to let go of her hand while I talked to him. He immediately brought a smile to my face.

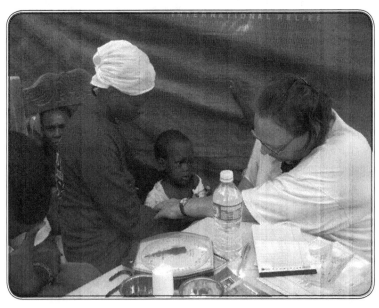

"Vicky was in triage and prayed with every blessed soul who came through the door."

"I don't know what will happen next, but I am thankful for a God who 'loves the little children of the world.' He cares for those little ones dearly in ways we cannot possibly measure."

"Good friends become better friends when you are in the trenches together."

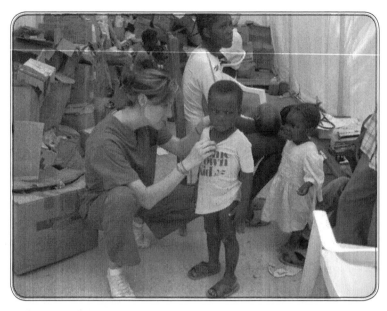

"My office was the tent I mentioned which had a large pile of what appeared to be garbage along one side . . . it was actually layers of medical supplies, clothing, and pharmaceuticals, haphazardly tossed in that space."

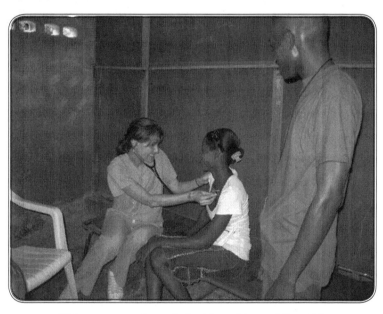

"When we were through, I said good-bye, adding, 'No matter what you choose, never forget—Jesus will always love you.' She smiled and said, 'I know He does.'"

Bobby and Lisa: what a team they were! "Did you ever meet a person who just seemed happy all the time?. . . Well, that pretty much sums up Bobby."

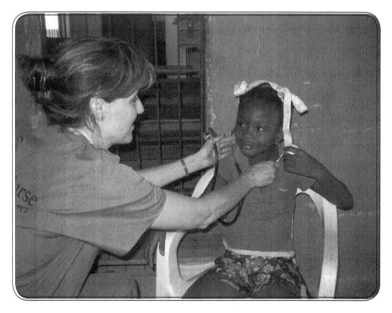

The kids got a kick out of listening to their hearts with my stethoscope, just as they do back home. This little girl is not letting the walls of her orphanage hold back her dreams. She wants to be a nurse when she grows up.

A beautiful view of the coastline from our van as we traveled to the clinic.
It is strikingly contrasted with the reality of the impoverished sites in the city.

The edge of a typical tent community. "I knew that things would look worse
today compared to my last there visit seventeen years ago—
before the earthquake."

". . . the sights gradually became more grotesque and destitute with each mile we traveled. Soon we were in the thick of the city. It was then that I remembered."

"I would love to tell you that I closed my eyes and cried out to God in intercessory prayer for them. But I didn't. I just plain lost it."

"Again, the destitute condition of these people just
slapped me in my rich American face."

"Forests were stripped of their trees, piles of rubble blurred the borders of what
appeared to be streets and communities, and makeshift tents were *everywhere*."

Garbage piles commonly pollute the water supply in the city. "'It's not fair,' I managed to squeak out. But in my heart, I was screaming, *It's not fair!*"

On closer inspection, you will notice that the material in the water to the right is made up almost exclusively of plastic bottles.

"We tell our children not to play in the streets, but here they are forced to build their makeshift tent homes on the road's median!"

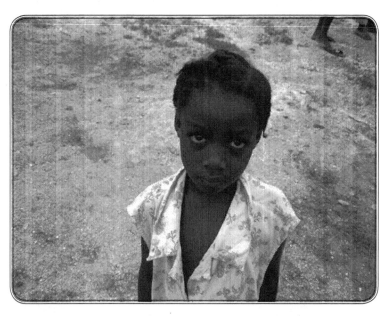

"I just can't shake those images. And do you know what?
I hope I never do."

Early morning outside the Cité Soleil clinic, "My favorite part of the day was listening to the pastor pray and sing with the patients before we opened the doors."

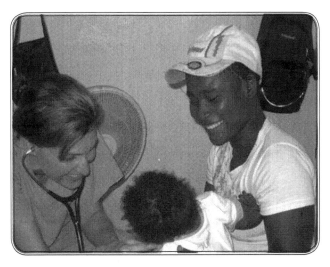

"That little soul, who had been so lethargic that she would not respond to me digging my knuckle into her sternum that morning, looked me right in the eye and grinned."

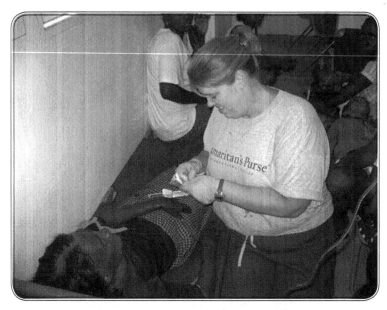

"... finally Lisa saved the day and got the IV in. I heard her exclaim, 'Thank you, Jesus!' and she really meant it."

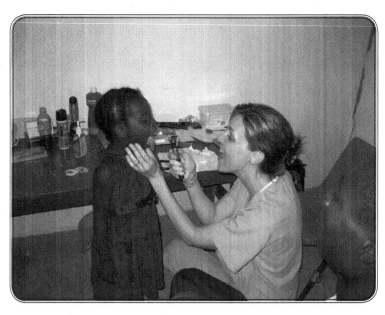

"Work at the clinic was busy again today. Still saw lots of kids (gosh, I love that part!) ..."

"It is amazing to see firsthand what a bunch of like-minded Christ-followers can do when given a clear mission. It's an honor to be part of it."

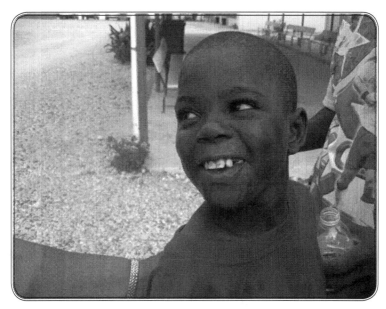

"Thank you, God, for saving Reginald. Thank you, God, for saving me."

He "ate two platefuls of dinner . . . I know because I cut up his meat and fed it to him. He was like a baby bird with his mama. He devoured that food!"

There is always hope. It lies in the Creator of that smile. "Don't tell me we don't live in a fallen world. But don't tell me that there is no hope, because there is. I know His name. His name is Jesus."

SUNDAY, JUNE 27, 2010

AT 11:30 A.M. today, it was over 110 degrees. I'm not sure of the exact temperature, because my thermometer won't read any higher. I don't mean to obsess over the weather here, but today was exceptionally hot! Right now, I'm thanking the Lord for the physiological gift of perspiration. But that's not why this smile is on my face. It is because of you.

Lisa and I were Skyped (can that be used as a verb?) today at church for the morning services, and the blessings we received from it have reached into the deepest parts of my heart. To even see the sanctuary brought tears to both of our eyes. Now, I am fully aware that the church is just a building, merely a thing. The Church of Christ is much more beautiful in that it is made up of His children internationally. But oh, the memories I have in that place abound! For Grace Bible Church is our second home. It is where I have laughed and cried countless times with so many brothers and sisters; it is where I sang for the Lord for the very first time; it is where Ed and I renewed our vows after ten rocky years of marriage; it is where we dedicated our precious children to the Giver of life.

As it is for many of you, it is the place where I have met to study and be amazed by the Word of God, to be taught by exceptional leadership, and to call out to the God of the universe in desperate need. It is where I have acted and danced on stage (did I just say "danced"?) and have had a blast with my closest friends. You are our second family, and we love you. I guess I knew that before I came here. But today, seeing you there seared it in my heart forever.

As I write tonight, I am reminded that I haven't really introduced you to our medical team. It is changing as we speak, with more people coming and going each day. Our smaller team is the one we have spent the past week with.:

By now, most of you know Lisa. She is my partner in crime from home and is a pleasure to work with. She is my type-A sister with OCD tendencies (which, of course, warms the cockles of my heart). She ran our pharmacy last week and did a superb job. She loves the Lord and is eager to serve Him.

Vicki is an ER nurse from North Carolina. She is a fairly new Christian and has a heart of gold. She did triage for us last week and prayed with each family we saw. She has shed many tears, taken at least 801 pictures, and kept us laughing when possible. Unfortunately, she left yesterday and headed home. When I think about her, I still smile. We miss her already.

Sue Ellen is a public health nurse, also from North Carolina. She is sweet-hearted, smart, and always willing to help in any capacity. She worked in the Cité Soleil clinic last week where Lisa and I will be serving starting tomorrow, so she is sharing pearls of wisdom with us today as we prepare.

Joy is . . . well, a joy. She is a retired OB nurse, originally from Trinidad, who now lives in Orlando. She is a West Indies version of my mother-in-law. (Mom, you wouldn't believe it!) She is gentle and kind, generous, and loves her family dearly. It is good to have her on our team.

You already heard about Dr. Trey. For you guys at work, he's kind of a cross between Dr. Scharf and Val. (Now that's an interesting combination!) There is also Dr. Gary, a family physician from the Geisinger area. He's all Dr. Burk. Gary is academic in his practicing, and very intelligent. To see him with the kids cracks me up. Here *I* am, being silly and putting my stethoscope in the kids' ears; and there *he* is, being so precise as he calculates their medication dosage just right. Actually, he is hilarious with his dry sense of humor and is tenderly compassionate with his patients. He is here with his son Mike, who is a college student in Michigan. He is considering medicine as a career. God bless Mike!

There are two more nurses due to arrive this week. We met one last evening named Sandy. She is a nursing instructor from California who will be joining Lisa and me in the clinic this week. We are in for another week of adventure, but we will not be alone. (Alas, there is not a nurse to replace you, Holly. I miss you desperately, but each day I am wearing the earrings you got me for Christmas. I haven't taken them off during the whole trip. I think of you every day.)

We are still unloading and organizing the medicines and supplies you all donated. I have told you of the surprise and excitement prompted by such a gift. I also have to tell you that because of that windfall, the construction crew had to build another set of shelves in our stock room! They now line both sides of our pharmacy, and our supply has been restored once again—so much so, as a matter of fact, that SP is able to fulfill another goal this week in its medical outreach: a *second* mobile unit at a remote location (Jack's Beach) about three hours from here. We briefly met their new team last evening and watched them drive off this morning. They will run a unit very similar to ours, and because of them, more souls will be touched and bodies will be healed here in Haiti. Thanks for being such an integral part of what is being accomplished here.

Sundays are relaxed for the most part here at the compound. We are all able to move a little more at our own pace, talk a little longer to each other, and spend a little more time reflecting on our experiences here. Some went fishing this morning (a very funny story), some took a van to the beach, and some used the pool here at the compound. I, however, indulged in one of my favorite things in life; I took a two-hour nap. I woke up in my ninety-five-degree room in a pool of my own sweat, but . . . ahhhh! I was rested and refreshed once again. The smile on my face will not fade easily—not today. As I close my eyes, I still see you all in my mind. My visit with you this morning, your encouraging e-mails, and your heartfelt, consistent prayers will keep us sane for another week. Thank you for being such a special part of my life.

Thank you, Lord, for family, friends, and heartstrings that withstand the distance of many miles. Thank you for my faithful husband who has taken on double duty these two weeks, all the while praying constantly for his wife. Thank you for my kids at home, whose childlike faith puts mine to shame. Thank you for my two moms, whose prayers reach the heavens as sweet words from their loving hearts. Thank you for friends, new and old, whose encouraging words are like medicine to my weary soul. Thank you for coworkers who are withstanding an extra burden in my absence; they never complain and are always quick to offer sentiments to bolster my confidence. Thank you for those who generously donated from our community. Because of them, Your work continues in spite of the depths of despair. And thank you for your Son, my Lord and Savior, without whom life here would make no sense at all. For only He brings true healing to those who are broken, and hope to those who are barren of spirit. You are, indeed, the Great Physician.

Here are a few last-minute thoughts as I leave you today—some things I have learned so far in Haiti:

- There is no such thing as maximum passenger capacity in a minivan.
- Duct tape really does have 101 uses. (Thanks, honey!)
- Toilet paper—don't leave home without it.
- There is nowhere on earth that God cannot penetrate, allow His presence, or provide for His people.
- Even feces-tainted juice tastes refreshing on a hot day.
- You can practice good medicine without HIPAA, CLIA, and malpractice insurance.
- The tougher the game, the tighter the team.
- Definition of a Haitian crash cart: an EpiPen, three outdated glucose tablets, and a rusty pair of scissors.
- Toenail polish can withstand a multitude of conditions.
- Boys have peeing contests in every tribe, tongue, and nation.
- Cold showers feel even colder when there is wind whipping through your shower stall.
- Good friends become better friends when you are in the trenches together.
- Even in a third-world country, I will find a way to use my curling iron.
- You can never cling too tightly to Jesus. Ever. (Thanks for the reminder, Ed.)

MONDAY, JUNE 28, 2010

WOKE UP WITH no water today. No, I didn't say no *hot* water. No *water.* And my watch stopped working. Oh, and my curling iron died. ☹

It occurs to me today that many of you may have had a lousy morning too. Some of you accidentally overslept for work. Some of you had cranky kids to deal with. Some of you are sick. And others likely had some Monday-related thing to do today that you dreaded all weekend.

As always, it is our response to such things that is telling. I don't necessarily mean our initial response. "Oh, no!" is honest. But once the reality of the fill-in-the-blank disappointment hits, *then* what do we do? Where is our heart? That's what God sees. And that's what He cares about the most. That is where the rubber meets the road between the response of the flesh and the response of the Spirit.

Hmmmm. I guess it's self-examination time again. Was I the *only* one without water this morning? Not only did the entire compound go without, but 95 percent of this country has no running water! Woe is me. And the curling-iron bit? Who ever heard of a bad-hair day in Haiti? Come on now. Our negativity can consume us if we let it, so let's just cut it out. We are blessed. Let's start acting like it. I'll try harder if you will.

Today was our first day at the Cité Soleil clinic. We saw 113 patients, mostly children. The clinic is different in many ways from the mobile unit. We have electricity, running water, and a toilet. (It doesn't flush, but after last week, it's an indulgence!) There are three physicians instead of two, and we're blessed with a greater variety of medicines and supplies. However on the flip side, overall the patients are much sicker. We started IVs on several of the kids and gave quite a bit of injectable meds today.

Of course, we are in the city now, so security is more of an issue. Our driver never leaves us alone on-site. We are thankful that the riots have diminished in the area, since the World Cup games have captured everyone's attention here. We are required to leave the clinic by 3:00 p.m. because of curfew.

All of this is in addition to our normal security routine. For example, we always carry a radio and cell phone with the team. As we leave or return to the compound or clinic, we radio the base with our whereabouts. (The guys on the team like to do the calling: "Code to base, this is Code 14, over . . ." It's a boy thing, and I am happy to let them do it!) We sign in and out of the compound, which is surrounded by several layers of razor wire and patrolled by guards with rifles. We each have a security badge and need to be prepared to show it at any time if asked. I was told that doctors are on the top of the list for kidnappings here, so I'm all for the rules and regulations! We appreciate all of your prayers for safety. Who knows how the Lord has already protected us?

The spiritual atmosphere of the clinic is also a little different. Each morning there is a long line of patients waiting for us when the team arrives. Many of them come several hours before the clinic opens its doors. A pastor leads a short devotional with them, followed by singing (I *love* to hear their voices) and a prayer. Inside the clinic, our medical team joins hands and prays together. Then we begin our day.

Each of us had our own stories to tell today. One thing I keep encountering is that children will often come in alone or with an older brother or sister. Their parent(s) are nowhere to be found. I met a four-year-old little girl today who came with her ten-year-old sister. She was filthy, poorly dressed, and her shoes were on the wrong feet. She had a fever, abdominal pain, and diarrhea. I not only couldn't get even a grin out of her, but she seemed devoid of *any* emotion. I wonder what she has experienced in her short life. What has she seen, heard, or felt that stripped the vibrancy of childhood from her? I didn't push the issue, she felt so ill. I just wonder.

Ed reminded me last night on his well-timed MP3 message that, although the people entrenched in this ruined environment appear to be helpless, there is a place that will never be destroyed, prepared by One who is eternal. He used Psalm 48 to encourage me, saying, "Even though the people of God may be surrounded by this devastation and destruction, we know there is a place that is indestructible and perfect, and *that* is where God is. What you see around you is temporary. But the glory of God is forever. And we, by the grace of Christ, will dwell directly in His glory someday." Well said, my dear. I needed that.

As I close up my day, I am rewinding in my mind to this morning's devotions. Our medical team discussed the fact that our goal here is not to be the most talented, the smartest, or the most gifted. It is about being willing to be used by a trustworthy God to serve Him in whatever capacity He chooses for us. Right now, we are here. We don't need to be perfect; He will put the finishing touches on us as we need them.

I love the fact that our team does not harp on the titles of "doctor" or "nurse." Yes, we have distinct roles and responsibilities, but each of us has been seen helping in the pharmacy, stocking empty shelves, and taking out the garbage. No one is better than anyone else. I have had the uneasy feeling over the past few days that some of you might be thinking, *I could never do what* she's *doing* or *All I do is_____. I haven't been to Haiti.* Now hold it right there. First of all, I'm just here for two weeks. Soon I will be home in my air conditioning, choosing my outfit for the next day from my closet full of clothes and eating ice cream for dessert as I complain about how cold it is! You know what I mean. I'm nothing special. And I'm not being a martyr. What I mean is that there are things about all of us that God chooses to use for Him. My "thing" is no more important than yours. This all started me thinking, mostly of the many things I admire about all of *you*:

- Sarah Beth S.—Your service to others is a blessing.
- Crystal M.—Your generosity puts us all to shame.
- Jennifer A.—Oh, if only I could sew like you!
- Joy B.—You put up with Steve (just kidding!), and you are a great mom.
- Ashley S.—I wish I had been where you are spiritually at your age.
- Darin Z.—I can't do Physics worth a lick!
- Mom P.—Your gentle and kind spirit is genuine and sweet. I know you make Jesus smile.
- Dawn K.—Your voice and your heart are beautiful.
- Melissa C.—I so admire the way you loved your Grandfather.
- Sally R.—Your smile lights up your face and always brings a smile to mine in return.
- Jason S.—You are a stealthy prayer warrior and bold for Christ.
- Lew Ann and Dwight K.—Your marriage is a testimony to us all.

- Dave—You, my big brother, were the first one in my life to show me what it really means to be committed to Jesus.
- Barb W.—I wish I could cook *half* as well as you!
- Deb H.—How can I thank you for the love of friendship you show to my Mom?
- Laura K.—You never have a bad word to say about anyone.
- Holly K.—You are one of my most favorite people in the world and the best nurse ever!
- Pastor Lou—You have caused me to laugh to the point of tears more times than I can count!
- Allisa M.—You would give your right arm to a child if you thought she needed it. You will make a *great* mom.
- Linda—You complete my brother and bring out the best parts of him.
- John W.—I admire your leadership, I and wish I were as funny as you!
- Shannon K.—You have the mind of an attorney and a heart of gold.
- Row—You are such a fun person to be around. I absolutely *love* your laugh.
- Penne E.—What *wouldn't* you do for your family?
- Michael S.—Your patience is remarkable.
- Pastor Todd—Your passion for Christ is contagious.
- Natasha K.—You are so good with people. You are in the right profession!
- Bonnie L.—Your insight into Scripture is inspiring.
- Aunt Pat—The great love and care you show to your mother is beautiful.
- Concetta S.—I could never take command of a classroom as you do.
- Ellen A.—Your commitment to your family is exceptional.
- Deb S.—I love to watch you praise the Lord in church.
- Leigh Ann K.—You loved your kids before you knew who they were. You were born to be a mom.
- Christine W.—Despite our differences, you still love me.
- Emily D.—Your passion for Christ is exemplified in your creative gifts.
- Jan G.—You never stop praying for your family.

- Sherry H.—You have inspired every blessed soul at Grace Bible Church.
- Aura—You are always so faithful to ask how I am doing, and you are patient enough to listen to my response.
- Jake H.—I love the way you love your mom and dad.
- Janice M.—You are faithfully carrying on your godly heritage. What a legacy!
- Pastor Daren—I will never have the wisdom to lead as you do. You are the earthly shepherd we desperately needed.
- Mom—You are so easy to love, and your love for others gushes out of you!
- Ed—Your faith and growth in Christ inspires me each day. You love me no matter what and make me a better person.
- Tina P.—Your boys will benefit for eternity from a praying mom.

So, there you have it. Your blessings flow right back to me. Thanks, all.

TUESDAY, JUNE 29, 2010

DID YOU EVER meet a person who just seemed happy all the time? People like this are smiling the first time you meet them, and that's how you always remember them because you rarely see them unhappy. They can be annoying in the morning, because they are singing when everyone else is trying to wake up. They find something funny that you don't—until they put their spin on it, and then you can't stop laughing. Well, that pretty much sums up Bobby.

Bobby was Lisa's interpreter last week, and he was our comic relief. And then, two nights ago, his twenty-five-year-old brother died. Just like that. He told Lisa afterward that his brother had been sick. Bobby works for a bunch of medical professionals, yet he has never asked for help. He came to work the very next morning, apologizing: "I might not be at my best." And now Bobby's greatest concern is that he doesn't have enough money to bury his big brother. We are working on that, but could you please pray for this young man and his family? He really does love the Lord, and he is such a hard worker. Life is hard enough here. Again, my fairness meter is going off the charts.

Work at the clinic was busy again today. Still saw lots of kids (gosh, I love that part!) but not as many of them were acutely ill. Lots of fever, diarrhea (I hope none of you just ate dinner), rashes, and abdominal pain—all in a day's work. But today we had some more serious social and spiritual matters on our hands.

One woman I saw today was named Angelina. She is a twenty-three-year-old woman who came in with chest pain, shortness of breath, and heart palpitations. Funny thing, though; it only seemed to happen when she was at home with her father. Further questioning revealed what I hoped it wouldn't. Her father is both verbally and physically abusive to her, often multiple times a day. She is a Christian and has friends and a church family to go to, but this woman is hurting in more ways than one. Her emotional stress is taking the physical form of panic attacks, and when she has them, she feels as if she will die. Some days she wishes she would.

Now, as you can imagine, psychiatric medications are not on formulary at our clinic. We are eternally grateful that we even have basic antibiotics, vitamins, and wound-care supplies. So my approach with her had to take quite a detour from where I would normally go. "I have no medicine to offer you," I told her. "The only thing I can give to you is the promise that the One you call Lord will never leave you or forsake you." I begged her to remember that although her biological father does not show her love, her heavenly Father *is* love and will always hear her when she cries out to Him for help.

I asked her if there was anywhere she could go to feel safe. Her answer was no. She has no way of supporting herself, and he is bigger and stronger than she is. I asked her if I could pray for her and then struggled for the words to say. I called out to the same God as hers, who had blessed *me* with a loving earthly father who would never have hurt me— the same God who had given *me* a happy childhood, parents generous with their love, and shelter from abuse. I felt so helpless—not just from a pharmaceutical standpoint but just in general. I mean, I'm a doctor. I try to "fix" things, either directly or indirectly. It's how I'm trained to think and react. But there was absolutely nothing else I could have done.

And then, during that prayer, I did something I rarely do in front of a patient. I began to cry. I could barely complete my last sentences; my heart just broke for this beautiful young woman. I was able to make it to "Amen," and then I lifted my head. And she was smiling. I'm sure the Lord knew I needed that. I know she has to go home to that guy. But thank heavens the Prince of Peace can give her the help I couldn't.

Another woman that will not soon leave my mind is Suzette. Suzette is three months pregnant. Her husband was murdered recently when their home was robbed. So now she is widowed, unemployed, homeless, and pregnant. Suzette wants an abortion. When I asked her why she doesn't want her baby, she couldn't stop sobbing as she told me her story. "I have nothing," she said. And she was just about right. The "just about" part is the rest of the story.

You see, right before she saw me, something happened to her in a stuffy little clinic in a ghetto of Haiti. A college student (Mike, from my previous entry) who loves Jesus decided to introduce her to Him. And she said yes.

Yes, she knew she had done things that would be warranted as sin. Yes, she knew that sin needs to be forgiven. Yes, she decided to believe that Jesus' choice to go to the cross to forgive her sin was real. And yes, three days later when that stone was rolled away, his tomb was empty. (The Beth Moore in me wants to shout, "Alleluia!" Thankfully, I'm a conservative, Baptist girl. ☺) Of course, after she accepted Christ she was still widowed, unemployed, homeless, and pregnant. But with God's Spirit and the local church ready and willing to help, she ultimately will not be defeated.

I prayed with her, reminding her that the decision she made to choose Christ today was the most important of her life. As we prayed girl-to-girl (with the help of my interpreter, of course), I said, "Lord, it's hard to be a woman. It's *very* hard to be a Haitian woman. It's *extremely* hard to be a pregnant Haitian woman." He knows. She kept crying as she listened to my words. I don't remember all of what I said, but when we were through, I left her with a final word: "Don't forget; you will *never* be alone again."

I gave her a month's worth of prenatal vitamins, and then I introduced her to the pastor who works with us at the clinic. As the Lord's providence would have it, one of our drivers (who was *not* scheduled to be there) was also able to speak with her. You see, his story and hers have a common thread in that his mother tried to abort him and failed. Now he is a Christian with a unique perspective on life. And today, God wove their paths together for a divinely planned conversation that began the process of her hope and healing.

So now, for lack of a better phrase, I'm pooped. It was a long day—and a good day. And tonight, I will rest in the arms of the One who lets some people die and others live. He lets some withstand abuse and others live in safety. He allows poverty and prosperity, hatred and love, pain and comfort. Don't tell me we don't live in a fallen world. But don't tell me that there is no hope, because there is. I know His name. His name is Jesus. Okay, Beth, you win. *Alleluia!*

WEDNESDAY, JUNE 30, 2010

SO HERE I am, sitting in my scrubs and flip-flops. I must be quite a sight! My skin is sticky, hair is everywhere, and I smell like a mixture of sweat, antiseptic solution, and bug spray. I have a cold shower written all over me. Before I take that plunge, however, let me share my day with you.

As we left the compound this morning, our medical director, Dr. Kara, broke one of the cardinal rules of medicine. She said, "Wednesdays are slow at the clinic. You should be home early today." Now, I know those of you in the health-care field are cringing right now. That's comparable to saying, "Hey, the ER isn't that busy" or "I haven't had an admission for hours!" Now ya did it. Oh well.

In any case, you guessed it. It was *busy*, and how! Don't get me wrong; I know that's why we're here. It is good to be busy, and those of you who know me well know that I do *not* like sitting around. It was just that the degree of illness was more intense today—so many hurting people. I saw things today that I would only see in the Intensive Care Unit at home. And here we are, desperately trying to manage them in a modestly stocked clinic in Haiti. Oh, and I found out yesterday that I was wrong about the running water. The sinks don't work.

My day began with a twenty-three-year-old man who was gripping his abdomen in severe pain. His temperature was 102 degrees, and he was so weak he could not stand. That would have been bad enough, but he had already been to the hospital over the weekend and was taking an antibiotic and pain medication—apparently to no avail. He was dehydrated from vomiting and diarrhea and had severe chills. The Haitian doctor was looking over my shoulder as I treated him and asked, "What would you do with him in the States?" I guess I was in work mode, because I'm afraid my answer sounded a bit brusque: "He at least needs a CT scan, a CBC, sed rate, IV morphine, and a surgical consult, but none of those are an option!" We did the best we could for him, and one shot, three antibiotics, and about four hours later, he was able to go home. We will see him again tomorrow—God willing.

Another patient was an eleven-year-old boy. He was brought in by his father, and the poor thing could not even stand straight due to his severe abdominal pain. His belly was as firm as a board, and his temperature was only ninety-five degrees; he was the first patient I have seen since I've been here who actually felt cool. I asked Sandy to start an IV on him as we contacted the nearest hospital. He had an "acute abdomen" as we call it—a true surgical emergency. He was slipping into shock right before our eyes.

Somehow the clinic manager arranged for transportation, and we shipped him off to the surgical hospital. Boy, was he sick. I think back on when my little David had his own surgical emergency at three-weeks-old. I remember asking his doctor if we could life-flight him to Pittsburgh. He looked at me with dead seriousness and said, "Chris, there's no time." I also remember witnessing my three-week-old Rachel coding in her hospital room, watching them rush in the crash cart and bag her little lungs with oxygen.

I say all of that to support the fact that I know what it is like to be a parent afraid for her child. Again, God uses our life experiences to be there for others. I would never have chosen to be the mom to experience such things, but these are things we don't get a choice about. The *choice* for us comes in what we do with those chapters in our lives. In any case, I quickly prayed with that boy and his dad as we waited for a driver. I begged God to get him the help he needed and to give his father strength. I wanted to go with them, but there was a long line of people waiting to be seen. He was only my second patient of the long day ahead.

As all of this was happening, a nine-month-old that Dr. Gary has been seeing since Monday was declining. Her typhoid test came back positive. She had already been treated for malaria and had been given IV fluids each day this week. Multiple attempts were made this morning to access her little veins, and finally Lisa saved the day and got the IV in. I heard her exclaim, "Thank you, Jesus!" She really meant it. I helped her tape and stabilize the line with a tongue depressor. We have learned to be very—how shall I say it?—*creative* here.

Unfortunately, this little one's condition continued to decline. She became more lethargic, her fever kept climbing, and the decision was made to admit her emergently. So once again we arranged for transport. I'm sure she was slipping into sepsis. In the States, it would be hit or miss. Here—well, I just don't know . . .

When things like this happen, whom do we blame? Because it certainly is a normal, human response to blame *someone*. We could blame the parents or the patient—*if only they had taken better care of their child or themselves*. We could blame the doctor or nurse—*if only they had been there sooner or changed their treatment plan*. We could blame the society or culture—*if only they had better access to health care, if only they weren't so poor*. We could blame the pharmaceutical company—*if only those drugs didn't cost so much, if only the company would donate more medicine*. And of course, we could blame the Big Guy himself—*if only He wouldn't be so unfair. He could have stopped it if He wanted to.*

Sound familiar? All of us have had similar thoughts, haven't we? They are honest reflections on an imperfect world. But blaming someone or something doesn't change a blessed thing. And chances are, that parent or doctor or company would never intentionally harm anyone. Sometimes bad things just happen. Are there bad sources behind those bad things? Yes. Are there neglectful parents, lousy doctors, and greedy businesspeople? Sure. But sometimes (let's all say it together now), "Life isn't fair." And blame is the fuel to a fire I don't want to burn.

We especially need to be careful when we begin to blame God. I know it is an honest response to this kind of stuff, but—blaming God? I don't know about you, but the Book I read about Him says that He started this whole world just fine. And when He made us, He knew full well that we would be able to choose to follow His rules or disobey them. Unfortunately, when we chose long ago to do it our own way, it opened a floodgate, which let loose a sea of consequences that we are still swimming in. But that same God never gave up on us. For goodness' sake, He *made* us, and He loves us more than we can ever imagine. We can blame Him all we want, but that doesn't change His righteousness one bit.

But it *does* feed our pride. What we are really saying is, "If I were God, I would *never* have let that happen." But you and I, we're not God. And we don't know the bigger plan, the broader picture, or have eyes that see into eternity. Guess who does. The One who put it all into motion.

Let's try and let Him do His job. And when bad stuff happens, and we can't see the sense in all of it, and it becomes overwhelming (I speak from experience), we can tell Him all about it and vent our frustrations. He can take it. And then we can ask for His help to humble ourselves and trust in the One who has a plan for us, the One who wants to give us a future and hope of His choosing. Oh, Lord, help my unbelief! And help me to trust in You.

THURSDAY, JULY 1, 2010

I'VE BEEN SITTING here for quite some time just staring at this blank screen. My thoughts and feelings are so scattered that I simply don't know what to write. This certainly is not my home, but in some ways, these two weeks have felt like two years. I don't mean to sound dramatic, but I do feel as if we have been here for a long time. And yet it has gone by so quickly. How is it that time can get away with such a paradox? I'm sure you can relate to that feeling at a particular season in your own life. What I *do* know is that my heart aches to be with my family. I miss them terribly.

I told Lisa today that I have a "switch," as I call it. I have mastered the use of it as part of my work. I began to utilize it in medical school, and now it has become a part of me. It is the switch, you see, that I need to hold in the "off" position when I tell someone they have cancer. I access it when I talk to the family of a loved one who is actively dying. It is the part of me that allows me to do what I do with compassion, yet it does not allow me to reach the degree of participation that would completely crush my soul.

I have been holding that switch "off" for my family while I am here. If I hadn't been, I would have taken the next flight home the day we arrived. But my grip on the switch is slipping, and I find myself letting my heart acknowledge just how desperate I am to see them again. I even began packing today; it was like therapy for me. I am finally allowing myself the realization that I will soon be home.

Speaking of home, I have talked with many people about the "readjustment period," as it's called. The last time I was here, I was twenty-three and single. I had no children, no car, and no job. I was a "poor" (in American terms) medical student with a boatload of debt, living in an apartment with bed sheets at the windows instead of curtains. Yet I clearly recall the moment I walked into that place; I fell to my knees and bawled like a baby. It looked like a palace. I remember being completely broken by the discrepancy between what I saw with my eyes and the images that were still vividly etched in my mind: "homes" made of cardboard boxes, wooden stakes with dirty rags hanging on them, and rusty metal roofs.

When I get back home, I ask you to please be patient with me when you ask, "How was your trip?" Because I'm really not sure just what I'm going to say to you. In any case, I am preparing my heart to leave Haiti and to reenter my life, realizing that these past two weeks back home have certainly gone on without me.

As they should have. My charts at work will be waiting for me, and I will no doubt have some patients who are angry at me for being away for so long. I will have mail to open, phone calls to make, and laundry to do. I will gladly step back into my role as Mom and enjoy catching up with the kids and their summer fun, allowing them to talk their little hearts out as they catch me up to speed. I will, no doubt, talk Ed's ear off into the wee hours of the morning, trying my best to share such a life-changing experience with my best friend. And now . . . I'm rambling. I told you I was all jumbled up!

My point is that I will step out of this experience and rejoin my life "already in progress." My prayer in this transition is that the Lord will allow me to take the best parts of my experience with me. As my mom e-mailed me today, her hope is that this all will make me a better Christian, friend, coworker, doctor, family member, mom, and wife—a better human being. That is my hope too. I want it to be intentional, not just a by-product of a trip. And that's something that will have to be a God-thing. If it were a Chris-thing, I'd be in trouble.

Work was busy again at the clinic today. I ordered more tests this time, mostly because the symptoms of the patients were just so varied. Saw some very high fevers for some reason today. Thankfully, no one was sick enough to be admitted to the hospital. (You probably gathered from my last entry that criteria for admission to a Haitian hospital is that you need to be on death's door.) The heat seemed more manageable today. I had to smile when I looked at the thermometer in my room. It read 94 degrees, and I felt comfortable! I think my thermostat will have some serious readjusting to do when I get home.

My favorite part of the day was listening to the pastor pray and sing with the patients before we opened the doors. As they sang, I found myself humming the beautiful but unfamiliar tune. I asked Eddie, my interpreter, what they were saying. "They say, 'Sweet Savior, Sweet Savior,'" he told me. They are poor, hungry, worn, and ill, yet their Savior is still sweet to them. Their faith is not circumstantial. Even when life is at its worst, the Savior is still sweet. Oh, how Jesus must have been smiling at them!

I don't have anything profound to say today. In fact, it occurred to me last night after writing my entry that what comes across in my words is likely very shallow. I'm no theologian, and I'm no author. I'm just some girl on a mission trip reflecting on my day. Please don't give me any more credit than that. You all have your own thoughts and opinions on your day that are just as valid as mine. I'm all at once surprised and humbled that you would even care to read my haphazard impressions.

Now, don't take this personally, but I need to tell you a secret: I would be writing this even if none of you were reading it at all. You see, it's like I *have* to do this while I'm here. It's as natural as breathing in and breathing out. It's how I try to make sense of the senseless things I witness here. It's how I try to organize the chaos of what I see. It's how I try to be honest with myself as I walk this road. And it's how I prepare my heart to have some very personal and gritty talks with God.

I need you to know that anything that has come across as remotely wise originated from the mind of God through His Word. Thank you, Lord, that it was my camera that was stolen instead of my Bible! It may sound silly to some of you, but I can't imagine taking this journey and staying sane without it. Anyway, I know that if anything of eternal value comes from this trip, it will be because He has ordained it. Otherwise, it was two weeks of, "Let's see just how hot and tired and homesick and worn out and emotionally crippled you can become before you break."

But it wasn't. It was two weeks of, "Let God show you just how amazing He can be, even in the midst of poverty, corruption, and apparent hopelessness, even as you are miles away from everything you find comfortable and familiar." He's so awesome. I hope I don't easily forget that.

P.S. I got to use the radio today . . . oh, I mean, I used the radio today. It's not like I really *wanted* to. Well, maybe a little. Honey, you would have been so proud. I remembered the call sign, the "over" and "out" and *everything*. And now, alas, my days as a radio operator are over. I think I'll retire as a lewtenent kerrnal . . . uhhh, whatever. ☺

FRIDAY, JULY 2, 2010

AT 5:00 A.M. today, I trekked up the hill, bleary-eyed and yawning, with bath caddy in hand and a towel wrapped around my neck. If you must know, I was headed for the outhouse, which is a little ways from our living quarters. I heard the now-familiar sounds of my second alarm—cows mooing, goats bleating, and a rooster crowing. But today an additional sound caught my attention and brought me out of my half-slumber—a baby crying.

Immediately I was taken back to December, and I got goose bumps all over. I found myself humming *Away in a Manger* with a smile on my face. What a precious reminder of our Savior's beginning—my Emmanuel (my favorite word, by the way), my God who came to be with us. Such a humble beginning was not far off from what I've seen here, and yet God chose a similar place as the location where He would physically enter the world. How simple. How beautiful.

As you can imagine, I have rather mixed feelings as I write this last entry. I am awfully thankful to be coming home, and yet I feel as if I've only begun to help these people. Or did I really help them at all? The image of stopping an exsanguinating aorta with a Band-Aid® comes to mind. I realize that if my sole purpose in coming here was to help sick people, then I have failed miserably. Oh, sure, our team saw over a thousand patients in these two weeks. We administered thousands of medications, put in long days, and experienced conditions that certainly tested our constitution. But if that was it, then that was it. If it had no eternal significance, then we *did* just put a Band-Aid® on the problem.

But if we were able to show these dear people a glimpse of Christ, or better yet to introduce them to Him for the very first time, then we have made a difference that no degree of poverty, disease, or depravity can wipe away. I can't help but think that I could have done more from a spiritual standpoint to help them. I think my discouragement stems from a particular patient today.

Claire is a nineteen-year-old woman who came in to the clinic this morning for a pregnancy test. Before she got through triage, the test read as positive. She burst into tears and was quickly ushered into my office. As I met with her, I learned that she was—you guessed it—single, homeless, and unemployed, had no mother or father, and wanted an abortion. She would not look me in the eye, and I was immediately crushed by the magnitude of her situation.

This was her first pregnancy—it was supposed to be different from this, right? She said that her boyfriend had already told her that if the test was positive, he wanted nothing to do with her unless she "got rid of the baby." Her aunt was willing to take her in, but not with another mouth to feed. I explained to her that we did not perform abortions at our clinic; we were there to help her, but not in that way. I asked if she was a Christian. She said she was not, and she did not want to know any more about such things. It was as if she was looking at me and saying, "Look, I came here for an abortion. If you aren't going to give me one, just leave me alone."

She did, however, let me pray for her. I wasn't quite sure how to do that, and I was actually surprised that she agreed for me to do so. I did the best I could. After we were done, she talked for a while with the office manager, Jasmine, who told me later that this young lady really didn't want to have the procedure, but she saw it as her only option. Jasmine acknowledged to Claire that she had a choice to make, but if she decided against the abortion, we would find a good home for her baby.

Claire left, telling Jasmine that she would think about the whole Christianity thing and might reconsider her decision about the abortion. I guess I didn't expect her to fall to her knees and thank me for being such a great missionary for her new Lord and Savior. But I was hoping to give her a divine opportunity to combat her obvious hopelessness and fear. As is true of us all, she will need to choose for herself.

On the brighter side of things, I saw the sickest child I have ever seen in my career today. No, really, it *is* the brighter side. At home, I would have life-flighted this nine-month-old to Pittsburgh. But today, circumstances being what they were, I started some oral rehydration solution, gave medicine for her fever, ordered a shot of antibiotic, and said a prayer.

A few hours later, in our "pediatric ICU" hole-in-the-wall, she perked up significantly and smiled at me. That little soul, who had been so lethargic that she would not respond to me digging my knuckle into her sternum that morning, looked me right in the eye and grinned. It just melted my weary heart. I don't know what will happen next, but I am thankful for a God who "loves the little children of the world." They don't always get better; they don't always survive. But He cares for those little ones dearly in ways we cannot possibly measure.

We had a debriefing tonight from the chaplain and his wife. They are kindhearted people who have been here since the earthquake and have quite a job to do. At the debriefing, they let the medical team do most of the talking; we discussed our initial expectations, the realities of what we experienced, and the good, bad, and ugly of what we will take back home with us. We have worked so well together as a team—a fact we are very thankful for. We are all anxious to see our loved ones again soon. We are grateful for what we did, and we wish we could have done more.

One thought that came up helped me to put a lot of this into perspective. When we leave here, we are not packing God up in our suitcase, taking Him home with us and away from this place. He will be coming home with us. And He will be staying here in Haiti. The reality of the omnipresence of God has always astounded me, but as we get on that plane and take off in the morning, it will have a stronger meaning in that moment. As believers, we simply cannot go where He is not (just ask Jonah). And among the people we have helped physically, as well as those whom we have impacted spiritually, seeds have been sown by us from the Father. And He will send more of His servants to water and nurture those seeds as He sees fit. How humbling it has been to be a part of the process.

So, as I wind down this journey, I would like to thank you all for coming with me. I really feel as if you have experienced much of this alongside me. Your encouraging words, constant thoughts, and faithful prayers have narrowed the distance between us and bolstered my determination to persevere. Really, you guys have been amazing. Thanks. I can't wait to see all of you (for some it will take longer than others) and let you catch *me* up on *your* two weeks. You have been so gracious to read about my journey, and I want to know how you are doing too!

I think it's the coolest thing that we will be arriving home on the evening before the fourth of July. If there was *ever* a July fourth when I will be proud and thankful to be an American, it will be this one. I'm not kidding; I'm kissing the ground as soon as we land in Miami! It's just that I have been in a place where everyone wants to come to the United States of America. Every single Haitian I have spoken with in regards to their hopes and dreams mentions America in some form or another. It *is* the land of freedom and opportunity. God has blessed us as a nation, and I am glad to be reminded of that. (Kids, be prepared; you are going to get a "proud-to-be-an-American" lecture from your mama. ☺)

So, as our team piles into the van one last time tomorrow, we will say good-bye to Haiti and this short chapter in our lives. I don't know what the Lord has in store for the future of this country or ours. But I do know that my faithful God sees this land through eyes of compassion and love that I can barely begin to comprehend. I know that our time here has had a purpose beyond my mortal understanding. And I know that in the future, my service for Him will take different forms, but it will never be in vain.

And finally, my last profound thought just before I hit the "Send" button is simply that I sure am glad to be coming home. See you guys soon. Oh, and don't stop praying quite yet. We still have a layover in Philly!

God bless you.

I love you all,
Chris

EPILOGUE

Experiences pass and memories fade. But as we go through these brief years, why not deliberately grasp the lessons God teaches us and incorporate them into who we are becoming? This will not only ensure that we grow, but that we remain teachable. My prayer for you is that the words I have penned will encourage you to purposefully pursue God's plan for your life and to actively take part in the journey He has designed uniquely for you.

This voyage may lead to your discovery of Him for the first time. It may spark your desire to read the unparalleled truth of His Word. It may prompt you toward service beyond what you thought you were capable of. Or it may just allow you to have a fresh perspective on your time here, remembering that there is more to this life than *you*. Yes, these things often lead us outside of our comfort zones. But go on—take that step. We are never alone as long as we follow the Leader.

When I consider the most common question I encountered upon my return, I find it rather peculiar. Why? Because although it takes the form of a question, it is actually more of a comment: "So, it really doesn't seem like things are changing there, does it?" Well, I suppose that depends on the type of "change" you are referring to.

As I have shared with you, the poverty and desolation in Haiti were more horrifying than many of us can imagine. And I am not naïve to the reality that many of the ill we cared for will have worsened. Some have died. Yet as I have described, I met hundreds of people whose lives had already been "changed" by the work of our host organization, Samaritan's Purse.

As a result of their work, I saw *firsthand* the freshly dug wells, medical care, shelter communities, and debris-free farmland these people have been given. Their world has been shaken, but they have a new beginning because a group of people, many of them just like you, decided to help the helpless.

But about this issue of "change" . . . if we limit the definition to *physical* change, we measure only what we can see with our earthly eyes. However, as this experience with SP taught me, when we filter the word "change" through the heart of Christ, it transforms the situation even further. He is very interested in our basic needs being met, but He is also deeply concerned with our eternity. He wants to give us more than hope of another day. He wants to give us Himself.

It is in the presence of *this* type of change where we stand in awe of God. For His brand of change goes far beyond what we are able to accomplish with planks of wood, bulldozers, and duffle bags full of medicines. It was not until I saw hope in the eyes of the desperate and joy in the faces of the weak that I realized that He was changing their situation well beyond the physical. He was changing them from the inside out. And in the process of my witnessing those glimpses of heavenly change, a byproduct of that process transpired—He was also changing me.

You may be curious about what happened after our return. As I write today, 321 days have passed since our arrival back home. I am sitting in my bedroom, typing on a laptop, with sunlight streaming into the room. Several birds are happily chirping the songs of spring outside the two windows behind me. My seven- and eight-year-olds are safe and sound at school, and my husband is downstairs cleaning the garage. I would not trade my time in Haiti for anything, but it *is* good to be home. As I close my eyes and reflect on my return last July, I recall it as a sweet homecoming.

After our return flight, Lisa and I had similar experiences at the Miami airport, in that we both began to cry when the officer stamped our papers and stated, "Welcome home." Our husbands were both waiting for us when we arrived at the State College airport, and my heart raced as I leapt into Ed's arms. I didn't think I could ever feel more loved. That is, until I saw my kids.

They were in bed when I got home, and I cradled their limp, sleepy bodies in my arms for who knows how long. I couldn't stop thinking of how beautiful they looked. They were so clean, so healthy, so safe. We attended church the following morning, and once again—yep, I bawled like a baby. I blame Michael, Lisa's husband, who is the worship leader at our church. He chose Chris Tomlin's version of "Amazing Grace" as one of our worship songs that day. How could I sing, "My chains are gone/I've been set free/ My God, my Savior has ransomed me . . ." without thinking immediately about Reginald? I was simply broken to bits yet simultaneously soothed by my merciful Redeemer. I'll never forget that day.

Two days later, I started back to work. I learned that one of our physician assistants, Liva, had completed every blessed chart for me, and that dozens more people than I realized had been following me along through my journal, cheering me on. They were careful not to flippantly ask, "Hey, how was your trip?" but instead gave me some time to readjust.

Soon Lisa and I were given an opportunity to speak at church about the experiences of our journey. We couldn't wait to thank those faithful saints at Grace Bible Church for their support in every way imaginable. Several months later, we heard of the terrible cholera outbreak in Haiti. I struggled to be practical, knowing I could not realistically go back so soon. Then, gradually, right before my eyes, my life settled back into normalcy. And although things by this point are pretty typical here in Central Pennsylvania, they will never be completely the same for me. This got me thinking.

As I considered how to construct a conclusion to my journal, I recalled a time seventeen years ago when I'd had similar reflections. At some point in your life, you have likely had them as well. They are related to the questions we ask ourselves after a significant life experience, such as, "How will this change me?" or "What long-term impact will this experience have on my life?" Sometimes we ask these questions and we don't wait for an answer. Sometimes we ask them and don't *want* an answer. And other times we ask them and then go on with life, not remembering we even asked them in the first place.

Well, today I allowed myself to remember. I still recall years ago when I pulled out my journal months after returning to medical school following my first trip to Haiti. I read it again today. I thought it would be fitting (and if I may be so selfish, therapeutic for me) to leave you with a few last impressions from my younger self. I can't help but grin at that idealistic yet sweet-hearted young girl at twenty-three as I consider what she wrote on the pages of that old, beat-up book. I smile, but not because she was mistaken with her impressions or because she was too immature to understand. I smile because she was changing. As I close, I thought I might share a few scattered thoughts of her young mind and tender heart.

In a world where I have lived for twenty-three years, I do not feel I have even existed—until now. Today I have embarked on a journey from which

I cannot return. Even if I had left this country the very day I arrived in it, I could never forget who and what I had seen . . .

Yesterday I woke up in an air conditioned apartment, in a soft, heavenly bed with familiar surroundings everywhere. Today I experienced a cruel, uncomfortable new world filled with pain, sadness, chaos, and fear . . .

I held the children, changed their diapers, fed them, and played with the older kids. How silly we must seem to them; we hardly know any of their language and must rely on *their* teaching abilities. Quite a role reversal. We learned songs, hand-clapping games, and new words in Creole. We did *not* learn how to leave a crying child after we had to put her down, how to laugh with a child dying from AIDS, or how to answer an orphan's question of "Where's my mama?"

I am drained, both physically and emotionally. I came here to do something, and I feel as if I am watching it all go by, as if it were a movie. But no one yells, "Cut!" And I cannot help. Not really. Why am I here? Maybe I will find out tomorrow. Maybe I will never know . . .

I felt the stares of the masses today, and they pierced my heart. I do not know what they are thinking, but it's hard to believe that they are not bitter toward us . . .

There is the smell of burning charcoal mixed with human waste; children and dogs pick through the garbage, and horns are blaring everywhere. Today I was standing at the top of a hill, looking down. I saw a great mosaic of colors and realized that they were moving. They were people. When I found out that we were about to become part of that crowd, I began to feel anxious . . .

I held an AIDS baby today. I'm not sure how to feel about it yet. She kept pointing to the window so I would carry her toward the light and tell her what I saw: "Look! There is a tree, a house, a woman—'*Bonjou, Madam*' . . . I hope you get to see these things someday . . ." But I knew she would not . . .

The abrasion covered his entire right arm, and the infection had already begun. I could feel myself shaking as I began to clean it . . .

I will never again be shocked at the performance of any driver on the road in the States. For today I have tasted death and lived to tell the story! I have not been afraid of anyone or anything since my arrival here, except for what occurs on the roads!

They were curious kids, hungry not only for food but also for attention . . . We try to talk with them, allow them to giggle at us, and hold their hands as we walk down the streets of their slum . . . It is heartbreaking. How will they survive? Many of them will not. The sewer they call their home will always be their prison . . .

Sometimes the evils of this world overwhelm me. That is, until I remember that I am responsible for many of them myself . . .

At first glance, it looked like a prison—a two-story cement building, cold, with ice-blue walls, filthy and overcrowded with men and women wandering aimlessly through its halls or moaning helplessly on their hard mattresses. But today God allowed me to see beyond that . . .

How will I ever be able to describe my experience here to my loved ones? How can I ever do it justice with words? I am thinking of all that I have done and how much remains to be done. I am recalling what I have seen and realizing that seeing is very different from changing. I would like to think that I will be more aware of the needs of others and become less self-centered, that I will want for less and strive for more, and that I will see people everywhere as God's children . . .

Maybe I am simply frustrated with the fact that life has to exist this way for so many people. It is primitive and raw. It is incompatible with a happy and healthy life. And it is very, very real . . .

When I got back to the house, I locked myself in the bathroom and cried so hard that it hurt. Despite all of the pain and confusion I have felt since arriving here, I had not cried once—before today. But the pain was too great, and I needed to let it out . . . And then I opened my Bible. How sweet it was to read the words again that Jesus spoke to His people . . . And once more, He carried me. That made all the difference . . .

I feel as if I have lived a lifetime since my first day here. At the least, I have experienced something that I will never, ever forget. In some ways, I am a new person . . . I suppose all things come to an end at some point. But soon it will be a beginning. I am excited and nervous at the same time. Yet it is another new experience for me to look forward to. I truly have a wonderful life.

———

Now that I am almost twice the age of that younger self, I can reflect on and affirm her words: "Well said, kiddo." I am humbled as I read those thoughts; how different I am and yet the same. One of my consistent prayers for years has been, "Lord Jesus, grow me up." I'm not there yet.

Nonetheless, by His presence in my life, He is producing growth. He matures my understanding of His truth by instructing me through His Word. He allows me to experience things that are impossible for me but possible through Him by leading me into service. And He reminds me that He will never leave or forsake me, as He hears my heart when I call out to Him in prayer.

My belief in Him does not add to or take away from His majesty; He is God whether I believe He is or not. But by honoring my faith in Him and developing my relationship with Him, He graciously calls me His own. He walks with me, at times to the point where I can almost feel His hand in mine. So, that twenty-three-year-old young lady *has* been changing. She doesn't love Christ the same as she once did. She loves Him more.

Praise be to God, whom words cannot describe, whose hope triumphs in our darkest hours, whose forgiveness penetrates the most wayward of hearts, whose glory declares His eternal majesty even in the depths of despair, whose grace blesses our most unmerited souls. Let me never forget. In the matchless name of Jesus, Amen.

Made in the USA
Lexington, KY
04 May 2012